Tejano
Music Award
Producer

MANNY R. GUERRA

ISBN 978-1-0980-5193-8 (paperback)
ISBN 978-1-0980-5194-5 (hardcover)
ISBN 978-1-0980-5195-2 (digital)

Original LOC Registration TXu 2-140-399
Library of Congress

Christian Faith Publishing, Inc.
832 Park Avenue
Meadville, PA 16335
www.christianfaithpublishing.com

Cover photo and photo enhancement by Jorge Flores / San Antonio, Texas

Printed in the United States of America

Dedicated to my 101-year-old mother
Lucia R. Guerra

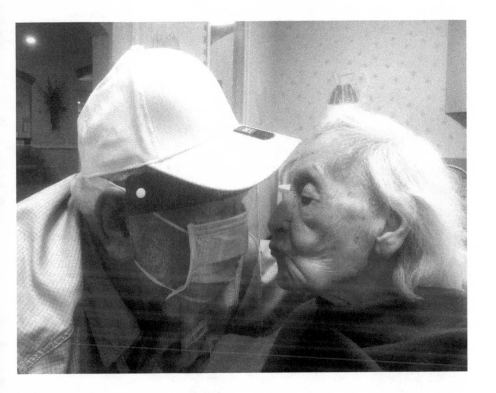

Acknowledgments

First and foremost, all honor and glory to Father God for His love and mercy and for the salvation of my soul through His only begotten Son, our Lord and Savior, Jesus Christ.

To my daughter, Gina Guerra Martinez, for her contribution toward making publication of this manuscript possible.

To my granddaughters, Taylor Martinez Olszewski and Skylar Perez, for their assistance.

To my wife, Rosalinda Guerra and my brother, Mario A. Guerra, for their help in editing this manuscript.

Introduction

My name is Manuel R. Guerra. In the Tejano music business, I am known as "Manny." From a modest family life on the southside of San Antonio to involvement in the Tejano music industry, including lucrative recording business ventures and ultimately, to the saving grace of Jesus Christ, my life has been an absolute roller coaster that has seen, heard, and experienced it all. I have lived in the simple and carefree environment of a humble home, felt the exhilaration of performing for large radio, television, and live audiences, experienced the stressful, high-paced aggressiveness of the high-dollar business world, suffered through the loneliness and despondency of a lifestyle that fills no voids and gives few, if any, reasons to continue to live and ultimately, graduated to a life filled with indescribable blessedness and a peace that surpasses human understanding. It is my sincere hope and prayer that the readers of this humble composition will learn from my many mistakes, benefit from my successes and most importantly, allow the seed of God and His Word, contained herein, to germinate toward the hope of eternal life in and with Him.

Early Years

On a Thursday, January 22, 1939, as the initial events of World War II were taking place on the other side of the planet, I was born to Manuel and Lucia Guerra. I was delivered by midwife in our home on Saldana Street, on the "southside" of San Antonio, Texas. Eventually, I attended Collins Garden Elementary and Burbank High School.

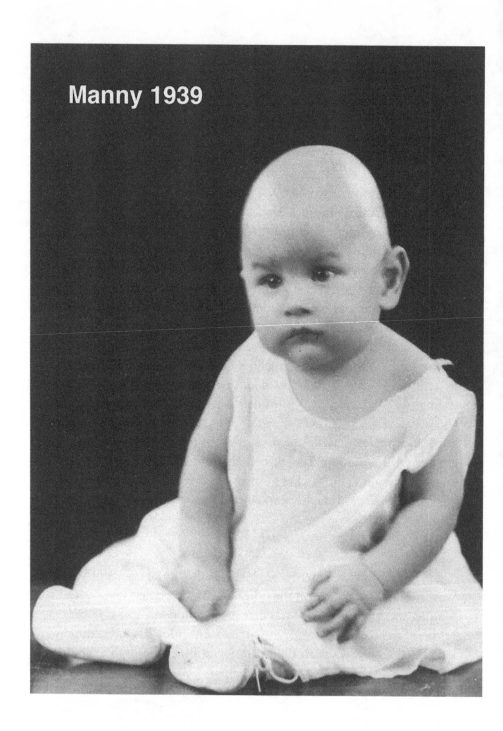

Manny 1939

My Exposure to Music

The Guerra home on Saldana Street was immediately adjacent to my grandparent's home, which was immediately adjacent to my uncle's house. That particular uncle, along with my father, established one of the first tamale factories in San Antonio, which came to be known as "The Tasty Tamale Company." The business began in a small building behind my grandmother's home (next door to our house). Although it was a part-time business, my mother and aunt would work at making tamales from the early morning hours through most of the day. My father and uncle promoted the business, convincing numerous local restaurants and grocery stores to serve and/or sell the product. The business steadily expanded and prospered.

Because the tamale factory was visible from a rear-facing window of our home, my mother would lay me in a crib by the window and was able to keep a direct and watchful eye on me while continuing to make tamales. In order to keep me entertained and to help lull me to sleep, she would use a radio for background music. Apparently, it was then when the music of the day, with its various styles, tempos, and arrangements, was embedded in my memory. Over the years, I found that music came to me quite easily and I am convinced that the consistent exposure to the music on the radio in my infancy was a major contributing factor. In fact, during numerous instances in my career, I performed "champagne music" (Lawrence Welk-type songs) that sounded vaguely familiar to me, although I never consciously recalled having listened to it prior to. Certainly that genre was not the type of music I was accustomed to listening to in my youth.

Manny 1941

My First Band

In 1946, at the age of six, I started my first band after having discovered that roofing nails on top of an empty tamale can produce a sound that is very similar to a snare drum. Soon the sounds of simple, improvised music lured neighborhood kids to our garage.

La Quinta Nuevo Leon

During 1951, my immediate family, along with an aunt and uncle, frequently attended what was known as "Tarriadas." These informal, family-oriented Sunday afternoon gatherings were held at a dance hall on Pleasanton Road, south of San Antonio and included live music, which was thoroughly enjoyed by all and never failed to prompt many to dance for hours. The music was conjunto-style, which consisted of an accordion, bajo sexto (twelve-string-type acoustic guitar), bajo (usually an upright bass), and drums. To my 12-year-old mind (and confirmed over the years), the gentleman on the bajo sexto was an amazing musician. Apparently, that particular gentleman passed his musical talent on to his offspring as well because, years later, I came to utilize his son's musical talents on many of my productions.

During the "Tarriadas," one could usually find me glued to the front of the bandstand, taking it all in. It was at one of these gatherings where I first heard the Perez Prado Orchestra's first recording of "Mambo No. 5" on the jukebox, during the live musician's intermission. I thought was it the most amazing sound I had ever heard. While the rest of my cousins were out playing and running around outside the big dance hall, I was visiting with the musicians, asking them questions about their respective musical instruments.

My First Musical Instrument

During that same year, I begged my dad to buy me an accordion, which thankfully, he did. At the age of twelve, I quickly learned three songs on my own. Thereafter, my parents and grandmother would frequently prompt me to play for family, friends, and neighbors. They were *so* proud.

One of my cousins was interested in playing guitar, so we started practicing together. Neighbors who heard us practicing soon began inviting us to play at their small family birthday celebrations. To the eventual annoyance of many of the adults, we proudly played the three songs we knew...repeatedly...for several hours. To our amazement, we were often compensated for our performances. We never could get over the fact that people paid us for doing something that was fun and that we loved to do!

Manny 1951

Hawaiian Guitar

Later that same year, people were canvassing the neighborhood, trying to convince parents to sponsor Hawaiian Guitar lessons for their children. The Hawaiian Guitar was an acoustic instrument and was played similar to the steel guitar of today, with the guitar placed face-up on the lap, using a steel bar on the strings. Since it involved music, I begged my parents to let me take the lessons. They consented but a few weeks after starting the lessons, my dad found the guitar laying in the driveway and he knew I had lost interest.

Piano Lessons

On or about the same year, piano became the next instrument of interest...and eventual disinterest. Once again, it was not difficult to convince Dad to dish out money for music-related lessons because in this particular case, my mother and sister also wanted to learn to play piano. Sadly, my interest in the piano lasted all of two years. However, Mom and my sister continued with their lessons, which served them well years later, in church.

Sunday School

I grew up in a time when the social club era was thriving. People became members of a certain club (there were several throughout the city) and would gather at Saturday dances, picnics, and other get-to-gethers. My parents were no exception. They avidly and regularly participated in the events. The following Sunday mornings, in order for them to catch-up on their sleep, they would allow a young pastor from a westside church to pick us up for Sunday school. This particular church was where my maternal grandparents attended for many years. It was at this particular church that I was exposed to a different type of music, traditional hymns. Sunday school was fun for me and the fact that I had "a school-boy crush" on the Sunday school teacher provided major incentive for maintaining my perfect attendance!

Junior High School

From 1951 to 1954, during my junior high school years, I attended Burbank High School. (Back in those days, the 7th through 12th grades were offered at the same school.) It was during those years that I started to learn to play the drums, which I very quickly realized was the instrument of choice for me! I worked extremely hard at learning to play the drums correctly and was rewarded for my efforts when the band director announced that I had qualified for the high school marching band (ahead of many of my classmates). This achievement, paired with my incessant, detailed, and colorful account of how my climb to "marching band fame" had transpired, very quickly overwhelmed my weary classmates' hearing and attention.

Membership in a Newly-Created Band

Even though the high school already had an "official" school-sponsored orchestra called The Melody Masters, other members of the high school band decided to form a separate band, independent of the school. In 1956, Julio Dominguez, the would-be leader of the band, who was also a trumpet player in the high school marching band, invited me to become a member. My unconfessed concern was that to that point, I had never played on an entire drum set, so I was not necessarily sure I would be able to do it.

Our first practice session was held at Las Palmeras Night Club, a dance hall owned by the would-be bandleader's father. The house drum set at the nightclub consisted of a bass drum and one ride cymbal. I quickly grabbed an empty beer box to use as a snare drum. After practice, the band leader informed me I would have to get my own drum set. This would come to be the humble start of the band named The Creepers.

My First Drum Set

Obtaining my new instrument of choice proved a bit more difficult than the accordion, Hawaiian Guitar, and piano lessons. Dad quickly made his feelings known: "I'm not spending any more money on any musical instrument for you!"

My response was "But Dad, this time it's for real! I really, really want to play drums!"

He said, "If you're going to play drums, you'll have to provide them for yourself. I want nothing to do with it."

My last and only hope was for me to run to my grandmother's house, explain my dilemma, and beg, "Please, 'Mamo!' Can you help me?"

Her response was, "Let me talk it over with your grandfather."

I went to see my grandfather about it a few anxious and nervous days later. He sat me down and said, "Your grandmother and I will give the down payment for your drums, but you will have to pay the balance yourself. You can make payments with the money you make playing with the band you're joining."

A few days later, my grandfather took me to C. Bruno and Company located on the corner of Broadway and Jones streets and there, we purchased the instrument of my dreams: a Ludwig drum set, complete with a bass drum, a snare, two toms, a floor tom, and multiple cymbals! I thought I was in heaven! Ironically and unbeknownst to me at the time, the salesman would later come to play a pivotal role in my life. His name was Phil Bushe, who, two years later, was hired as the band director of the Burbank High School Marching Band.

Latin Music

As a teen-ager, I was drawn to "Salsa music," which in my day was referred to as "Latin music." As a fifteen-year-old, I was able to spend a summer in Santa Clara, California, attending concerts at the famous "Rainbow Ballroom," listening to world famous Machito & His Orchestra, Tito Puente, and many other famous Latin groups. I also listened to The Fania All-Stars out of New York City. My favorite vocalists during those days were Graciela (Machito's sister) and Cuban-born singer Olga Guillot. My first love was "Latin music." Later in life, when I became a music producer, I was well aware of the fact that I would not survive producing that type of music, particularly in Texas. The demand was just not there. Consequently, we would go on to adapt our music to our very specific environment.

First Gig

Throughout 1955, The Creepers played at Las Palmeras Night Club every Friday and Saturday night. We played Quincy Jones, big band-type music, which was popular at the time. Soon, I was able to begin making payments on the drum set like I had promised my grandparents. Also, it was at that time that I married my high school sweetheart. Life was good!

Having spent many hours "hanging out" with fellow musicians, it didn't take long for me to be tagged with a nickname. My father's well-known nickname was "La Borrega" (The Lamb), which he received because of his curly hair. Since the bandleader's father knew my dad when they were younger, all it took was for him to call me "La Borregita" (little or young lamb) once in front of the other musicians and from then on, that became my nickname.

Manny 1955

Johnny Sarro Orchestra

After playing at Las Palmeras for over a year, another popular orchestra led by Johnny Sarro, which played Spanish music and Pop songs, asked me to join their band. Although I was very reluctant to leave my high school friends behind, I accepted the challenge to take a step up; the compensation was certainly better. I played with the Johnny Sarro's Orchestra for about two years, when yet another orchestra leader requested my services.

The Emilio Caceres Orchestra

In 1958, I received a call from renowned bandleader Emilio Caceres, asking if I was interested in joining his orchestra. Fortunately, when he called, I was not aware that Mr. Caceres was famous. In fact, I later learned that he had been named "America's First Jazz Violinist" in one of the editions of the "*Who's Who in Music*," an annual, national publication that provided music-related information on all genres. Had I known of his fame at the time he called, chances are I would have gotten cold feet, with fears that I would not have been able to perform at his level.

The Emilio Caceres Orchestra catered to a completely different type of audience than I had known to this point in my career. Similar to genres I would play later in my career, Mr. Caceres' music was Big Band/40s type music…but with a Latin flare. Additionally and unlike many bands of the day, Emilio developed and provided written musical scores for use by the musicians, which resulted in "tight and clean" musical sounds. It was normally a ten-piece orchestra but extra musicians were hired for bigger gigs. To have the responsibility of maintaining control of the tempo for such a large group of professional musicians was unbelievable to me. Ironically, years later, Mr. Caceres would come to play a pivotal role in one of my music-producing ventures.

The Jack Skiles Trio & The Larry Herman Orchestra

In 1959, at twenty years of age, I joined The Jack Skiles Trio, which played at an exclusive club at the Petroleum Center in San Antonio. The appeal of playing for this trio was that they were a house band, which meant less travelling…and…they played soft, contemporary jazz and Frank Sinatra-type American music, which was different from what I had played up to that point; so, I had the opportunity to learn a different genre.

After playing with The Jack Skiles Trio for several months, I received a call from Mr. Larry Herman, leader of The Larry Herman Orchestra, asking if I would be interested in joining his band. Mr. Herman was an accomplished pianist who later became the owner of the popular Roaring 20's Ballroom in San Antonio. I jumped at the chance to play "40's big band music." We played at the St. Anthony Hotel every Wednesday through Friday. On Saturdays and Sundays, he would book the band at venues throughout San Antonio and surrounding areas.

As a member of this band, I gained quite a bit of experience and was blessed to learn many wonderful life lessons. As the only Hispanic in the band, I never felt any discrimination from any of the other band members, which was truly ironic because this was also during the same era that teachers would report anyone caught speaking Spanish in the school halls, often culminating in suspensions. Remarkably, my bandmates took me under their collective wings and taught me about the music business but more importantly, they showed me what it was to have and live with integrity. Learning this lesson came to be an essential element in my future musical successes.

The Isidro Lopez Orchestra

In 1959, I became a member of a band from Corpus Christi, Texas known as The Isidro Lopez Orchestra. I joined this band because they traveled throughout the USA and my thoughts were that I would be able to continue doing what I loved, while also being able to explore the rest of the country. During my tenure with this band, I was confronted with multiple, life-changing aspects of life that I had never before experienced. The larger world around me was now different from what I had known before; my world had changed…and it was changing me. Gradually, my life had progressed from playing music with fellow high schoolers to being a part of the "music business" and all of its trappings. It all brought about a dramatic change of lifestyle from what I had previously known, both professionally and personally.

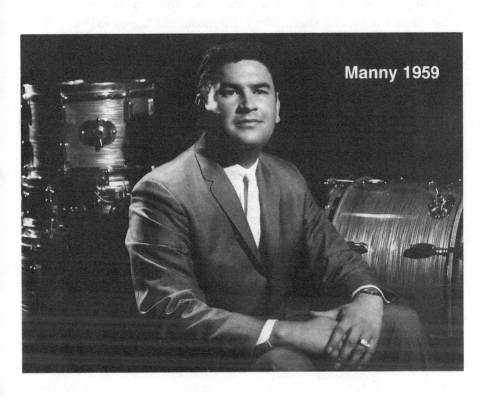

Manny 1959

My Mother's Conversion

In the summer of 1960, after giving up on life, my mother attempted suicide by ingesting a large number of pills. While in the hospital emergency room, specifically while having her "stomach pumped," she recalled thoughts about the God she had heard about during her childhood. In those moments, she prayed to God and apologized for making such a mess of her life and she asked Him to allow her to die. Later, when she recounted her experience, she recalled that God gave her an alternative to her request for death: He prompted the thought that if she was finished living her life and wanted to give it up, He would gladly take it over. Thinking that she had absolutely nothing to lose, she considered His offer. At forty-one years of age, she accepted the Jesus Christ as her personal Lord and Savior. Since then, she has dedicated and lived her life solely with God as her priority. "At the time of this writing, my mother is two months removed from 102 years of age." Her testimony has led hundreds, possibly thousands of souls to the feet of the Lord Jesus Christ; some directly, through her own ministry and others, indirectly, through the ministries of some of her children and others who have also come to serve God because of her faithfulness to Him.

A New Start Up Group

Before leaving The Isidro Lopez Orchestra, I began to help a musical group started by Sunny Ozuna and my younger brother Rudy, by booking them at venues through dance promoters I had met throughout the years. They called their band, Sunny & the Sunglows.

Manny 1961

MANNY R. GUERRA

Sunny and the Sunglows

In 1962, I became the drummer and bandleader of Sunny &
the Sunglows. The band proved to be very popular and very successful! Our first record, written by Sunny, was titled "Golly Gee" and
was released on the newly-established "Sunglow Record Company"
label, which came to be the first of numerous record labels I would
own. This recording made it possible for us to sign a recording contract with Columbia Records ("Okeh") label.

Sunny and The Sun-Glows   Columbia Recording Artists

Talk To Me

In 1963, we recorded a song titled "Talk To Me," written by Joe Seneca, a composer and movie actor. Several groups recorded the song prior to us, including Little Willie John in 1958, Bobby Vee in 1960, and Lloyd Price in 1962. (The song was also recorded by Boz Scaggs in 2015). Our particular version and recording of the song, including the violin arrangement by Emilio Caceres, reached the top national chart position on *Billboard, Cash Box*, and *Record World* magazines, the music industry's most recognized trade magazines at that time. "Talk To Me" enabled vocalist Sunny Ozuna, a Burbank High School student at the time, to be a guest on "Dick Clark's *American Bandstand.*"

On the record label:

SUNGLOW
RECORD COMPANY

3207 S Flores St

San Antonio, Texas

Violins & Arr. by
Emilio Caceres

2:41

G 110 A

Unknown

TALK TO ME
(Joe Seneca)
SUNNY
and the
SUNGLOWS

Cutting Edge

Sunny & the Sunglows and later The Fabulous Sunglows, proved to be a creative, innovative, "cutting edge" group. We were the first to initiate inclusion and use of the electric piano (1962), the Hammond B-3 Organ (1963), a live violin section (1963), and a Synthesizer (1972) in our recordings. The thought processes that prompted inclusion of the electric piano, organ, and violins were for enhancement of the particular arrangements and sounds. The idea behind the use of a Synthesizer was to overcome concerns related to poorly-tuned brass and woodwind instruments with a synthesized sound that was perfectly-pitched.

Rhythm and Blues (R&B)

Our generation had great Rhythm and Blues (R&B) recording artists like James Brown, Wilson Pickett, Little Richard, Ray Charles, The Drifters, The Coasters, Bill Doggett, and others. The musical styles of those great artists also had an influence on the music we created and recorded, which was actually a "fusion" of and closely tied to the different types of music we grew up listening to. In fact, Sunny & the Sunglows had the opportunity of recording at Cosmo Studios in New Orleans, which was the home-studio where "Fats" Domino recorded most of his hits. Our first two single records (45-rpm) in Spanish ("Pa' Todo El Año" & "Voy Sufriendo Por La Vida") were recorded there.

The Sunglow Record Label

The "Sunglow Record Company" produced artists that included Conjunto groups like Los Pavos Reales, Flaco Jimenez, Toby Torres, Joey Lopez y Los Guadalupanos, Clemente Bermea, George y Maggie, Cha Cha Jimenez y Los Chachos, and many others.

My career as a record producer allowed me the opportunity and privilege of placing five different recordings on the Top 100 Charts of the best-known music trade magazines in America. Those recordings included "Golly Gee" and "Talk To Me" by Sunny and The Sunglows, "Guess Who" and "Peanuts" (La Cacahúata) by The Fabulous Sunglows, and "Iron Leg" by Mickey & The Soul Generation. The long hours of work and focused effort resulted in successes and achievements that were certainly enjoyable and gratifying...but they came at a steep price; I was divorced in late 1963.

Chicano vs. Tejano Music

During the early to mid-70s, two popular record labels claimed to be from the "Chicano Music Capitol" of the world: one was from New Mexico and the other one from Texas. Numerous musical groups were referred to as "Chicano" bands. However, by current definition, their music could more accurately be classified as Conjunto or Norteño music, simply because their lead and dominant instrument was an accordion. While we were initially classified as "Chicano music," the music performed by The Sunglows could not be easily categorized into any of the genres of the day. We merged, altered, and fused a combination of American Pop music, R&B, Salsa, Conjunto, and ballads, along with progressive musical arrangements of classic and current Mexican songs. Of note, the "Chicano" designation or term originated from and was more closely associated with political viewpoints and discussions of the day. Because of that and a number of other reasons, I opted to use the term "Tejano music" to describe our progressive, fused-type music that for the most part was predominately listened to and enjoyed...by Texans.

The Seed is Sown

After Mom's conversion to Christianity, she would continually invite me to attend church with her. She would say, "Son, Jesus died for you and He wants to save you. He is the only One who can help you fill the emptiness that exists within your soul. He alone can satisfy that thirst." "Poor Mom," I thought. "She means well but she has lived her life and had her fun and now there isn't much for her to do, so she spends all her time at church. Surely no young, successful person like me would be wasting his time there.

One day, I decided to have a serious talk with my mother to set her straight on this religion thing. My dad and I were opposed to how she and her religious chatter were negatively affecting the family. By our way of thinking, she was becoming a religious fanatic! Not even the neighbors were coming around anymore. All she talked about was Jesus and salvation. We cautioned her to back off, telling her it was not good to be so obsessed with these things. "All religions are the same," I would say.

A few days after lecturing her on the ills and negative effects of religion, she responded by hanging a sign in the living room that read: "No smoking inside this house." It wasn't a big deal to me because I didn't smoke but it was, in effect, a declaration of war for my father, who smoked two packs per day. The Guerra house had now "officially" become a war zone! Up to that point, we had jokingly referred to it as "the Jesus thing" but now, Mom had just gone too far. She was attacking Dad right where it hurt him most. Dad and I got together and agreed that this was just too much. She was violating people's rights by imposing such a rule. After all, she did not pay the rent, Dad did! What's more, Dad was the head of the house; the final authority! But all of that tradition didn't seem to faze her one bit. She stood firm in her convictions and replied, "If you have to smoke, you'll have to do it outside, because there will be no smoking in this house." I thought this would be Mom's downfall; ultimately, her undoing. She had done this to let the whole family know how serious she was about the things of God. As occurs with any situation when the proverbial line is drawn in the sand...and subsequently crossed, from that day forward, our home became Mom's battleground for proclaiming and testing her Christian faith.

Just like the Bible warns, the hardest, most difficult trials a "believer" can experience take place in the home, between family members...and our home was no exception. My mother went through some trying, heartrending, difficult times with and because of loved ones under the same roof. Using her new life in Christ as a weapon against her and only because it inconvenienced us and our lifestyles, Mom endured our injustices, insults, and the constant mocking of her faith for many years.

The Pains of Success

While we were celebrating and enjoying the popularity of "Talk To Me," Sunny was encouraged by a Houston promoter to leave the group and start his own band. When Sunny did, in fact, sever his ties with the group, many viewed it as having dealt a devastating, fatal blow to the group. We all wondered, "How can a band survive with no vocalist?" To make matters even more difficult, my brother Rudy also opted to leave our band to join Sunny in his new band. This particular point in time proved to be a dark, disappointing, and difficult time for me. In fact, I remember wondering if my career in the music business had come to a sudden end. I recall praying to God, (even though I was not even sure He existed), "If you're really out there, let me know if I'm in the wrong business and I'll gladly seek a job elsewhere."

The Fabulous Sunglows

Our band *did*, in fact, recover from our vocalist's and Rudy's exit. That same year (1965), we began performing under the new name, The Fabulous Sunglows. With the idea of presenting and promoting a re-packaged band to the general public, we decided to go into a local recording studio to record a single 45-rpm record, featuring one of our two new vocalists, Bobby Mack. The song we chose was titled, "Guess Who," a song Jesse Blevins had recorded some years prior. A month after the release of the single, while in Dallas for a gig, one of our band members banged on my motel room door that Saturday morning, yelling for me to turn the TV on to Dick Clark's American Bandstand. To my surprise, they were playing "Guess Who." Two weeks later, the single made Billboard's Top 100 listings.

We continued working on an album with Bobby Mack and our other new vocalist, Joe Bravo. When we realized that completion of the album was going to take some time, we decided to release another 45-rpm single, specifically for radio play. In those days, radio station disc-jockeys (DJs) would often take it upon themselves to play whichever side of the record they preferred. They would often flip the A-side (usually reserved for what we thought to be "the better song") and would play the B-side (usually used to provide "a less preferred song;" a filler). In order to eliminate that possibility, I *strategically* decided to place an instrumental on the B-side, which, I reasoned, would result in the DJ having no choice but to play the A-side, "Fallaste Corazon." *Fortunately*, my "clever" strategy didn't work!

While on our way to Austin for a performance, we stopped to greet Ricci Ware, a popular radio personality at KTSA in San Antonio at the time. He asked if we had a new follow-up recording yet and I told him we had just released a single record, but that it was in Spanish. I added, "The B-side is an instrumental." "Let me have it," he said. Ricci, for reasons known only to God, opted to play the B-side! The rest, as they say, is history. The instrumental on the B-side, titled "La Cacahuata (Peanuts)," ripped through all the pop charts and became a huge success for us. The song was later recorded by Herb Alpert and the Tijuana Brass and by the Lawrence Welk Orchestra.

At that point, I felt like everything we did, as far as music was concerned, was going to be a success. I was certainly proud of our accomplishments and I felt I had grasped all the world could offer. On the relational side, I had begun my second marriage, so there was much happiness. However, from my professional achievement/ gratification perspective, something seemed to be missing. The more successful I became, the deeper I felt a void within me. I began living life in the fast lane. I turned to alcohol and diet pills for amphet- amine-like stimulation. I just could not figure it out. It was like an unquenchable thirst that would not or could not be satisfied. Nevertheless, I continued to perform as the group's bandleader and drummer until 1968.

My Venture in the Retail Music Business

In 1965, I opened a small record shop in the 3200 block of South Flores Street on the southside of San Antonio. For the most part, it was an opportunity to make our recordings more readily available to our fans. Because we had not yet recorded long-play (LPs; 33-rpm) albums, I would bundle four or five 45-rpm records in a package to meet and satisfy demand.

Religion Infiltrates My Own Home

During my second marriage, Mom was able to convince my wife to trust in the Lord Jesus, so now there were two Christians trying to change me! When my wife began attending church up to three times a week, I complained that it was too much church. Soon, however, I figured out that when my wife was at church, it was easier for me to slip out of the house. So, from that point on, I decided that my wife should not miss *any* church services.

From the moment Mom "got religion" (as we referred to it), there was no letting up on me. She regularly mailed me nine- or ten-page letters. She was determined to, one way or another, tell me about the things of God. I would read the introduction to the let- ters up to where she started talking about Jesus, then I would fold them and hand them to my wife. She would ask, "Did you read your mother's letter?" I would say, "Yeah, some of it. It's just too long." I gave them to her to place in a drawer with the other previously-sent and partially-read letters.

Dad Threatens to Leave

One day, having grown tired of hearing about religion, Dad informed Mom that if she continued trying to change his way of living, he would leave the house. Shortly after he voiced his threat, I happened to stroll in, happily celebrating my birthday. I walked into the house with gifts that friends and fellow musicians had given me. I quickly saw the expression of disapproval on Mom's face as I unwrapped one gift in particular, which I immediately realized was the wrong gift to have shared. It was a complete traveling liquor dispenser set. Dad was happy that my friends were so thoughtful but Mom said, "It isn't enough with what you're doing to yourself by drinking. Now, even your friends are helping to destroy your life?!" That was the straw that broke the camel's back. Dad's immediate and heated response was, "If you continue to embarrass and humiliate our children like this, pretty soon, they are not going to come around to see us anymore! Instead of bringing us together, you are dividing us!" Thereafter, the environment was fairly thick and heavy around the house for a few weeks. My thoughts were that the woman was possessed.

Whenever I was not on the road traveling to the next gig, I would often eat breakfast at Mom's. It never mattered what subject I would talk about, she would give me time to say my piece, then she always managed to shift our conversation to the things of God. She never let up, telling me that I needed salvation and that I needed to be "born again." As I reflected on Mom's new life, I was thoroughly convinced that she had been completely brainwashed. She was totally dominated by the church she attended and by "*that book*" she was always carrying. "How can a person let a book change their whole way of thinking?" The only logical conclusion, I thought, was for me to take it upon myself to rescue Mom from the evil influences that had taken control of her. I confidently set out to explain to her what her problem was.

"Mom," I said, "'*that book*' you believe in and live by; have you ever stopped to think how many people were involved in writing down all that information? Being human, they must have unintentionally made some mistakes, which are now misinforming you!" She was quick to show me in 2 Timothy 3:16, where it reads, "All scripture is given by inspiration of God, and is profitable for doctrine, for reproof, for correction, for instruction in righteousness."

"Well, that's fine, Mom," I said, "but what if the person who wrote that part was wrong? What if he is sharing what *he* considers truth? Anyway, how can you trust in something that was written so long ago?"

The answer she gave me made me realize that there was something more here than I could understand. *Mom could not possibly be smarter than me*, I thought. I knew the illustration she gave me came from an extraordinary source. It was simple but it was enough to knock me off my soapbox.

"Son," she said, "when you went to Chicago for the first time to perform, how did you get there? How did you know exactly where the city was?"

"That's easy," I said, "we just stopped at a service station, picked up a map, and we were on our way."

She asked, "Did you ever stop to think about how many people were involved with putting that map together?"

"Thousands," I confidently answered.

She continued, "Did you ever think for a moment that any one of them could have made a mistake and given the wrong information about the roads leading to Chicago?"

"Well, I get your point," I said, "but we got to Chicago, didn't we?"

"Yes, son," she said, "in the same way, the Bible, which is God's Word, will lead all of those who trust in His Son Jesus Christ to eternal life."

I was speechless.

Thereafter, Mom would tell me that the talent God gave me was for His use, honor, and glory. I remember snapping back at her once concerning the music business. I said, "Look Mom, my business provides employment for many people, including me. I have responsibilities. Who will support my family, God? Do I just stop everything and expect it to rain money from heaven? It is easy for you to serve God because you don't have to provide for yourself; that's Dad's responsibility! You have nothing else to do but spend your time in the church and make our lives miserable with your religion. Is your church going to support my family? Ask them! If they are willing to do that, I will sit alongside you in the church, doing whatever it is you do!"

During the following weeks, I searched for the hardest questions I could come up with to get back at her. I asked a variety of questions and she would always answer directly from the Bible. One day, I asked her, "How can you be so sure that if you were to die this very moment, you would go to heaven?" She answered, "God has promised eternal life through His Son Jesus Christ. It is through *faith* in our Lord Jesus Christ that we are saved and will inherit eternal life."

"Aha!" I said, "So all you can answer to this question is to say we have to have faith. Every time I come up with a good question, you use the same answer about having faith. When you can't prove something, you always give me that faith business. I knew you wouldn't be able to find all the answers in that book. I guess I was right. You are going to have to give me more than that."

Her face saddened as she said, "Son, for some time now, I have been talking to you about God's truths, so you can come to the knowledge and saving grace of our Lord Jesus Christ, but you continue to belittle and mock God's Word. From this day forward, if you want to know what the Bible has to say about *anything*, you can look it up yourself." She closed her Bible and left me sitting at the dining room table, stunned and dumbfounded.

Mom and my wife continued to pray for me but I continued living life under my terms. After all, it was *my* life! I had every right to live it to my own liking!

MANNY R. GUERRA

My First Recording Studio

The building that housed my record shop had a bicycle shop next door. In 1966, when the bicycle shop side of the structure became available, I rented the whole building and I cut an opening through the common wall, combining the two large rooms. That was the start of my first recording studio which, a couple of years later would come to be known as "Amen Studios."

Amen Recording Studio

As soon as I had decided on and taken action to establish a recording studio, I *borrowed* a mono Ampex 350 one-track tape recorder and purchased a used broadcast mixing board, which had no equalization capability. Since it was a "one-track" machine, I had to record entire bands or orchestras at the same time. If a mistake was made anytime during the recording, even if immediately before the end of the song, we had to stop and start again "from the top." Having "no equalization capability" also meant that the device had no controls for me to be able to control or adjust sound frequencies of those being recorded, which produced a "flat" sound similar to music that has had the treble and bass controls all set to "zero." A tavern across the street from the studio gave me a used extended jukebox speaker that I used to monitor the sound.

Although I had been a part of many recording sessions as a musician, I began my recording studio with no actual hands-on experience as a sound technician. However, through the years, I did notice that the quality and sounds we recorded at professional recording studios never reproduced or sounded the same on the finished vinyl record. The fidelity and quality never seemed to transfer to the manufactured side. I was intrigued by the question and challenge of whether it was possible to reproduce and transfer true sound onto a vinyl record.

Since my recording studio was in its infancy, I started my business by recording small, young bands that were just starting out in the business. From their perspective, they were happy to know that a recording studio was willing to give them a chance. On my part, there was no pressure; I was just trying to prove to myself that I could learn and acquire the sound technician skills to be successful in the business. Within two years, my studio had upgraded to an Ampex 4-Track recorder and a Gately mixing board.

Necessity: The Mother of Invention

As I continued recording and producing music, local bands that came to the studio, including many from across the country, all seemed impressed with the sound, which I was continually focused on improving. However, because I did not have the funds to purchase newer, more current recording equipment, I had to improvise in order to make up for the deficiencies. One of the deficiencies that I had to contend with was the inability to create and add echo to music recorded in the studio. Several experienced recording technicians had informed me that the larger, established studios had special echo chambers that were built to specification to reproduce natural echo, which was basically accomplished by feeding sound through a speaker on one end of the chamber, thereafter recovering that sound through a microphone at the other end of the room. The cost to build an echo chamber to specifications was very expensive and was certainly out of my price range.

One day, as I was driving to the studio, I happened to see a huge underground gasoline container being towed into a yard for metal salvage. I stopped and asked the man towing it what they were going to do with it. He said, "We cut them in half and sell them to ranchers to hold cattle feed." He sold them for $150 each. It measured about eighteen feet in length and was about six feet in diameter. I told him I would buy one if he would place it on my property, to which he quickly agreed. Because of limited access to the property behind the studio, it took the driver nearly an entire day to place it where I needed it. I remember him saying, "If I had known how much trouble it was going to be, I would have given you the container and charged you $1,000 to move it!"

Once the tank was cleaned and prepped, I placed a speaker at one end of the tank, a microphone at the other, and eagerly piped sound into my makeshift chamber. Amazingly, the sound I received was clean and clear. Thereafter, I hung partitions inside the tank to reflect, diffuse, and delay the length of the sound waves, which allowed me better control for recording purposes. I was extremely happy with the results. When word got out about the echo chamber, recording studios from Dallas and Houston sent their recording engineers to see what I was doing. I must admit that more often than not, I was somewhat embarrassed at showing folks the gasoline container that now doubled as my echo chamber, although, I was genuinely happy with the wonderful echo it produced. The only downside to my use of the storage tank is that it could not be insulated, which occasionally required me to redo some of the recording mixes…because of the dogs barking next door.

Saved by Grace

In May of 1968, I visited the Free Methodist Church where my mother attended, which was two blocks away from her home. Mainly, I went out of curiosity; to check it out. Certainly, my intentions were anything but honorable. At the close of the church service, they sang a hymn. The melody hit me. In fact, it stuck with me all that day. Dismissing it as nothing more than an emotional experience, I, nonetheless, decided to check things out a bit further the following week.

During my second visit to the church, the songs again brought a lump to my throat, to the point that all I could think of was "*Let me out of here!!*" It was the strangest feeling I had ever felt. However, I managed to compose myself and when the church service was over, I did, in fact, rush out of there. This odd feeling, I determined, was all in my head. Fear possessed me. I did not know what it was. Curiously, I gathered enough courage to go yet a third time!

It was Sunday, June 2, 1968; I told myself that I would move up a few pews and listen to every word spoken by the preacher, from the beginning of the message to the end. My intent was to figure out what was going on with me. As I listened to the opening song, that now familiar feeling came over me again. I tried to fight it off but something started to move within me, giving me a strong urge to cry. I vainly resisted with every ounce of strength I could muster. When the song was finally over, I quickly managed to get back in control. I listened intently to the person presenting the sermon and halfway through the message, I knew *someone* more powerful than the person on the platform was speaking. Even though I had believed that I was really something special, I suddenly realized that I was the poorest man on the face of the earth. A great power was urging me to go forward but the speaker was still preaching. *Finally*, the minister gave an invitation for those who wanted to receive the Lord Jesus Christ as their Savior to come forward.

I wanted to go but suddenly it seemed like my feet were bolted to the floor; I couldn't move! Somehow, I managed to take the first step and then, thankfully, I was able to make it the rest of the way. With tears streaming down my face, I knelt at the altar and asked God to forgive me. I confessed *my need* of His Son Jesus Christ and I received Him as my personal Savior. As the rest of this document will attest to, we are to come to Jesus humbly, desperately seeking and reaching for the only hope we have for salvation from eternal damnation. "Humbly" means that we come to Him so He can take over the reins of our selfish hearts; so He can sit on the throne of our hearts to rule our lives as He deems appropriate, not as we think it should be. Being saved and continuing to live as we want, with no repentance and no change, with us at the wheel instead of Him, is not salvation; it is nothing more than a humanly-based refocus of the same sinful heart, mind, and life that desperately needed Jesus in the first place. After I left the altar and took my seat, I shared with a person sitting next to me of the emotions that filled my heart and how wonderful God was. As I walked out of the church that morning, for the first time, I saw flowers, trees, and people driving by like I had never seen them before. It was as if I had been blind and now I could see. It seemed like someone had taken a black-and-white world and converted it to full, vivid color.

I soon realized that the songs I was so moved by during the church services were sown in my heart as a little boy. My grandparents sang those same songs in their church. It brought to mind fond memories of my youth. A certain young minister had made it his mission in life to pick my sister and I up, so we could attend Sunday School. He drove quite a few miles from the church that he pastored to our home. He did that *every* Sunday. Mom recalls that on many occasions, the only thing the young minister saw after he had stopped in front of our house was a hand waving through the window, indicating we would not be going to church that Sunday. Thereafter, this gentle soul would drive back to the church with an empty station wagon. Not once, did he ever complain. He just kept coming back Sunday after Sunday, for years, until we became teenagers. The seed of love this dedicated servant of God sowed in our lives was now being reaped in my life. This day was truly "the beginning of the rest of my life." "Therefore, if anyone is in Christ, he is a new creation. The old has passed away; behold, the new has come." (2 Corinthians 5:17). "…so shall my word be that goes out from my mouth; it shall not return to Me empty, but it shall accomplish that which I purpose, and shall succeed in the thing for which I sent it" (Isaiah 55:11). The "*seed*" that my precious mother had consistently sown for close to nine years proved what God says is true, "it shall not return to (Him) empty."

The Following Sundays

The Sunday following my conversion, I dragged 125 visitors to church. Most of them came out of respect for me, as their music producer. My intent was for them to have the same spiritual experience I had received. The Sunday after that, only eighty visitors showed up. After a few more Sundays, only about ten showed up, although they continued to visit for the next few months.

During the first few months after my conversion, I still had the band, but I decided to hire a drummer to take my place on the band's forthcoming gig in Chicago. I did not want to miss the three weekly church services, which were too few to my liking. I wanted to be there all the time. I began to read the Bible from ten to twelve hours a day. I could not get enough. I felt a conviction of having to make a change in the production of secular music work that I was producing.

Recording of Testimony

After I was "born again," I wanted to share what God had done in my life with everyone I came in contact with. I *owned* a recording studio, so I decided to record my personal testimony. I did the first LP album in English and the second one in Spanish. I never sold a single copy. I gave them away to everyone I knew in the music industry.

One day, as I walked into the record pressing plant, the owner asked if I had a minute to discuss something. This gentleman and his wife played pivotal roles in helping me establish the recording studio. They always encouraged me and had even agreed to co-sign on a "start-up" loan with me. While in his office, he said, "Manny, you haven't paid anything on your account and your current balance is already up to a few thousand dollars." I explained to him that I was now doing God's work and it was important for me to use these recordings to reach people. He leaned back in his chair and calmly asked, "Are you telling Mama (his wife) and me that God has given you an outreach to share about the change that has taken place in your life...at our expense?" I was stunned and embarrassed. At that very moment, I realized I was solely responsible for the financial cost of delivering the recording of my testimony. That day, I resolved never be a financial burden to anyone for the "calling" God had placed on my life.

Amen Records

I established the Amen Records label in late 1968, after my conversion to Christianity. The first recording I released on the label was the first Christian song I had ever composed, "Yo No Soy De Aqui." I knew no gospel singers at the time, so I asked Joe Bravo, lead singer with The Sunglows at the time and Clemente Bermea, who was signed to my secular record label, if they would record it for me. Thereafter, all the gospel music that I recorded was released on the Amen Records label.

The label is still active at the time of this writing. However, in 1990, the name was changed to Amen Music. All of my brother Rudy's gospel recordings are on Amen Music. Musical groups and/or song interpreters on the label include: Los Unidos (Houston, TX), Matias, Joe Kino (Arizona), Los Truenos de Tejas, Kiko Alvarez, Los Hermanos Reyes (Guatemala), Maria Elena, Joshua y Los Amiguitos, Hosanna, Ricardo Montoya, Jimmy Edward, Voz En Zion, and others.

Recording of Judgment Day

A year after accepting Jesus Christ as my Savior, the Lord inspired me to write a drama of a man who died and found himself before God at judgment. It was titled *Judgment Day.* The main character in the drama *thought* he had lived a good enough life on earth and that he was "okay" with God. However, every time he responded with an explanation to God's questions regarding details of his life, God simply countered with appropriate scriptures from His written Word. The compelling drama was intense and ultimately ended with the sinner being cast into the "lake of fire" (i.e., Hell) for eternity.

Realizing that I personally was not capable of providing the rich, bass voice one would commonly associate with the voice of God, I placed it in God's hands, through prayer. Shortly thereafter, while waiting at the service counter at a local record pressing plant, I heard a voice speaking in a baritone/bass tone. I walked over to him, introduced myself, and I asked him if he was in the record business. When he answered that he had done some radio commercials, I asked him if he would be interested in reading a script at my recording studio. Two days later, I recorded his voice, edited, and mixed it into the master tape recording. A few days after the recording was completed, while a photographer was visiting the studio, I decided to play the recording for him. After he heard it, he became very upset and said, "That is a very negative recording." Based on his response and because I was a new believer in Christ who did not want to offend anyone, I filed the master tape away, where it remained for ten years.

One day, while searching for a particular tape, I happened to come across the *Judgment Day* tape. I placed it on the machine, listened to it and thought, "This should not stay on the shelf. It should be out where it will make people think." So, I released the cassette tape and it achieved extensive circulation in the local and regional area.

One night, while working late at the studio, I received a telephone call. I wondered who might be calling at that late hour. I answered the telephone and the person on the other end of the line asked, "Is this Amen Studios?"

"Yes," I answered.

The caller asked, "Is Manny Guerra around?"

"Yes, this is he."

"I am calling from California. Do you have a minute?"

I responded, "Yes, of course."

He continued, "My wife and I recently moved into this house where I am calling you from. We have been in cleaning mode. While my wife was in the attic, she found a cassette tape that was left behind that, apparently, you recorded. It's titled *Judgment Day*. I just want to tell you that after listening to it, we prayed the prayer you recorded on it and we received Jesus Christ as our Lord and Savior."

I was astounded! God proved He is love, He is all-powerful, and that distance between where He shares the seed of His Word is absolutely irrelevant to where He makes it fall and take root. He will find the lost souls He seeks and bring them to His feet, according to His sovereign Will.

Special Friend

In 1965, three years prior to surrendering my life to Jesus Christ, I met the owner of small, corner grocery store that was not more than 50 yards from my recording studio. Through the years, he and I became very close friends. He knew the life I lived prior to my conversion to Christianity and a few days after my conversion, I shared my new life with him as well. He thought it was likely a phase I was going through and was not impressed.

Throughout the years, my friend was always ready to extend a helping hand by aiding me with cash loans. He never doubted that I would repay him and trusted me enough to not make it an obligation. After my encounter with the Lord Jesus Christ, one of the first things God prompted me to do was to repay my friend all that I owed him. I went into his grocery store a few days later and informed him that I was going to pay him what he had loaned me over all those years. He laughed and said, "My dear friend. You will never be able to pay me what you owe me. Don't worry about it." I responded, "Please look in your little black book and tell me what I owe you. I will be back tomorrow." I went back the next day and asked if he had determined my balance?" He said,

"It has always been in the book. It's on top of the desk; you can see it for yourself." I opened up the little book and was stunned to see a balance of $24,000! My first gut-wrenching reaction was, "Lord! What have I done? I shouldn't have asked!" God immediately impressed on me that I was doing the right thing."

Offer for the Purchase of the Sunglow Record Label

Toward the end of 1968, I prayed and asked God if it was His will for me to sell the Sunglow Record label, to help me find a buyer. Oddly enough, at that particular point in time, I had begun to question my decision to trust God with my life. I was not aware that the Bible teaches that God will not eliminate believer's problems. However, He *will* provide the true believer with strength, focus, and peace that surpasses human understanding to go through those problems. From my inexperienced and uninformed perspective, He was not making things very clear, which gave me a tendency to lose faith. After having turned my back on the world that had given me innumerable business opportunities, here I was, experiencing nothing but trouble and grief for my efforts. After leaving behind my life of sin and joining the church, I expected God to speak clearly of what He wanted me to do and how He wanted me to move forward. I had not yet learned that God gives His people all the guidance they need on how to live, how to make decisions, and how to prioritize... through His Holy Scriptures. Because of my lack of adequate study of the Scriptures and because I did not feed on His Word for guidance, strength, and spiritual sustenance, doubt began to creep into my mind as I gradually realized things were not going to work out the way *I* had assumed they would. The joy of my salvation began to diminish. I was very troubled, discouraged, and emotional.

My emotional misery was interrupted by a knock at the door. I quickly wiped away the tears from my face and went to see who was calling. I partially opened the door and saw a man standing there. I asked him how I could help him. He asked if Manny Guerra was in and if he could come in for a moment. Reluctantly, I let him in. This person had heard about my recording business and seemed to know all about the

Sunglow Record Company label. He was from California and said he had followed my career through the years, had heard the news of my religious conversion and that I wanted out of the record business. He further stated that he was visiting a mutual friend in San Antonio who had told him I was interested in selling the record company and he thought he would stop by to verify if the information was correct.

"Do you want to sell?" he asked.

"Yes," I answered.

"What is the asking price?" he asked.

"I don't really know. I haven't given it much thought."

"If you could give me more or less an idea, the company I represent might be interested in buying it," he claimed.

Unable to control my pounding heartbeat, without giving it much thought, I blurted out, "Twenty-five thousand dollars!"

He calmly responded with "That seems like a fair price." "May I use your phone?"

"Of course," I answered.

He talked, in private, for a few minutes then came out and said, "In two or three days, the president of Certron Corporation, Record Division, will meet you here at the San Antonio Airport. He will give you a retainer/deposit until we finish the proper paperwork on your company. If everything is in order, the corporation will send you a check for the balance within thirty days."

I tried to keep my cool but it must have been obvious to him that I was in shock. I could hardly wait for him to leave so I could fall to my knees and ask the Lord to forgive me for not trusting Him. However, as I prayed, I could sense that something was still not right. I remember thinking, "What am I missing, Lord?" I am sure you sent this man here today. Why am I not at peace?" As I began to re-think through the casual conversation that had quickly progressed to negotiations, I focused in on and started to question my blurting out a price, without having considered all things. In order to counter my mounting concern, I reasoned that the dollar amount was a lot of money; certainly, more than what I thought the record label was worth. As I stopped to pray about it, I decided to take a look at the accounts payable information for the business. When I reviewed the books, I quickly and shockingly realized that twenty-five thousand dollars would not be close to being enough to cover the record label's debts. Here I was again, up against a test…this time, of my own doing! My dilemma caused me to be concerned; very concerned. However, as I continued in prayer, I felt a peace and confidence that God would see me through this. I knew that God had the power to make *anything* happen; I believed in Him. I just had no clue *how* he would do it. It was certainly a test of my newly-found faith in Him.

As I continued to pray about it, I knew that at some point, my only recourse would be to call the interested party to tell them I had made a mistake. I was embarrassed and very reluctant, but I knew that now that I was aware of the true costs, I had to be honest with them. The next day, I dialed the telephone number that I had received. I immediately recognized the voice of the man who had come to see me. I started to speak and began to stutter. I was unable to make myself clear.

He asked, "What's wrong?"

I said, "Remember when you asked me how much money I wanted for the record label? I told you I did not really know and I gave you a random, non-informed figure off the top of my head. Well…that figure is wrong. I need to get forty thousand dollars."

His stern answer was, "I don't think so, Mr. Guerra. You gave me a price and we agreed."

I countered with "The record label can't be sold unless I pay its debts. That is the amount of money owed to the creditors."

He said, "I can appreciate all that but that is your problem. I do not think my associates will appreciate what you are doing. I will get back to you." He hung up.

The 4:30 AM Change of Heart

While visiting my parents' home a few days later, I heard voices arguing as I was approaching the front door. Mom was talking to Dad about something that was very upsetting to him. As I entered and saw Dad walking toward their bedroom, I asked Mom what was going on. There had been a disagreement over a decision one of our family members had made that had upset Dad and he was now not willing to open the doors of his home to that family member. Apparently, my paternal grandmother had also been involved in the argument. It was quite a scene.

I sat at the dining room table after things quieted down and Dad came in and sat at the table. I asked him if he was okay. He said, "If your mother does not respect my decision, I will leave." As I listened, I could hear the hurt in each of their voices and sensed the hurt in each of their lives. I said, "Dad, if God Almighty was to deal with us as we deal with those we say we love, there would not be much hope for any of us. We are talking about family." As I was leaving via the back door, I passed through the kitchen and heard Mom praying. She said, "I know God is going to bring healing to this situation."

That night, during the early morning hours, the sound of a soft cry woke me. At first, I thought it might be a dream. However, I heard it again, as if the cry was coming from close by. Fear came over me as I tried to listen more closely to the crying sound. My heart sank with every cry. I got up from bed and glanced at the clock; it was 4:30 AM. As I walked into the hallway, I heard the sound coming from the children's room. As I entered the room, I found one of my children weeping. It was a cry of someone who, it seemed, could not be comforted. I prayed for my weeping daughter, as well as for my other children. At that moment, I thought about my dad. I told the Lord, "If this is your way of revealing something, then prepare me for what is to come."

Later that same day, when I visited my parents' home, Mom greeted me at the door and said, "Your dad left you a note on the dining room table." As I opened the note, the first thing I saw was what was written at the very top of the page; it read: "To my son Manuel, written at 4:30 AM." *Why would Dad bother to put the time on his note?* He wrote that he had reconsidered his decision and would allow the loved one to return home. I praised the Lord for His loving kindness and mercy.

My Best Friend

My father was the best friend I ever had. He was a very important figure in my life. I kept nothing from my dad. He knew more about me than any other person in the world. When the world left me brokenhearted and lonely, he was always there for me. He always supported me and made me feel like he was proud to have me as his son. I loved him very much.

One of the hardest things I have ever had to do was to respond to a request made by my dad. Mom had been talking to him about her concerns with sending my two youngest brothers to the store for cigarettes. She was trying to raise my two youngest brothers in the knowledge and teachings of God and going to the store to buy cigarettes was not something she wanted to continue. At that point, my dad turned to me and said, "Here, son, you go and get me some cigarettes." I loved him so much that I would do anything for him… *but I froze.* I did not know what to say. I looked at him and with all of the courage I could muster, I said, "Dad, I love you very much, but I cannot do this for you." Without a word, he turned and walked away.

Several months later, while I was having breakfast at my parent's house, Dad began having difficulty swallowing. As he got up from the table and went into the bathroom, Mom told me the problem was getting worse. He had not been able to swallow solid food and was now having difficulty swallowing soup. My father was a strong man who had never experienced a serious illness, so he did not seem too concerned about the situation. However, as the problem continued and worsened, Mom decided to take him to the doctor. The doctor's initial diagnosis was emphysema. He gave Dad some medication and sent him home. However, Dad continued getting worse. Soon, he returned to the doctor and after further analysis, the doctor recommended that he see a specialist, just to be sure. Mom made the appointment for the following week.

A Counteroffer & A Doctor Visit

It was during those days that I again received a call from the Certron Corporation of California. They were now offering thirty thousand dollars for the record label. It was not good news for me because I knew the companies I owed money to would not grant me a release. The caller asked for my decision. I said, "No, it is forty thousand dollars that I need, but thank you for your consideration."

We hung up. At that point, it really didn't matter much to me because my priority and focus was on my father's health.

We kept the appointment with the specialist and Dad entered the hospital for diagnosis. He was there for three days. On the third day, as we were preparing to take him home, Mom said the doctor wanted a word with us. The doctor was brief and to the point. He said, "I have the results of the X-rays and other tests. Your dad has inoperable cancer of the lungs. He has, *at most*, six months to live."

There is never any way to prepare for something like that. I prayed, "Dear God, if this is your will, then give me the strength to accept it. I do not understand it, I do not like it, but there is nothing I can do about it." We started Dad on regular cobalt treatments, but they didn't help; his cancer was too far advanced. His forty years of smoking had taken their toll. The hardest thing for us to see was my dad experiencing difficulty breathing; his lungs were failing.

My Father's Passing

During April and May of 1969, Dad's condition worsened. Mom continued to share Jesus with him and sang spiritual songs as he lay in the bed. It was during this illness that Dad surrendered his heart to our Lord Jesus Christ. His last days were a true testimony to his friends who came to visit at his bedside. On Sunday, June 8, 1969, eleven days before his fifty-third birthday, he went to be with the Lord.

It was amazing how God could turn such a somber, depressing event into a time of celebration. Although Dad had just recently been saved, he came face-to-face with our Lord Jesus Christ...before any of us. I praised God for the way He truly filled us with "the peace that surpasses all understanding" (Philippians 4:7) during that time of trial and grief. Members of our family who did not yet have a personal relationship with God found my behavior disrespectful. It was disturbing to them to see me glorifying God through the horrible experience of losing my father. For me, it was an occasion of unspeakable joy, which family members and friends mistook for a form of happiness. (Happiness is a state of mind, while joy is the state of a peaceful heart filled with faith in Jesus Christ.) Because hundreds of people attended the church service and burial site, we were able to share the message of Jesus Christ with many non-believers. People who would have otherwise never attended church were exposed to and heard the Gospel because of my father's passing. Praise the Lord!

As the father of two well-known Tejano musicians, the news of Dad's passing spread quickly. The news reached Certron Corporation. I received a call from them the next day informing me that they had reconsidered and would pay the forty thousand dollars. The record label was sold for the exact amount I needed. However, somehow, none of that mattered at that moment. Instead, I prayed to God for strength in the months that followed. I knew God was with us, in the midst of our suffering.

Regarding the music business, I did not know what I was going to be doing once the sale of the record label was completed, since there would likely be a non-compete clause in the sale contract that would prevent me from starting another record label. So, I dedicated myself to increasing the gospel recordings on the Amen Records label. Over a period of a few months, I became aware of quite a few people that were serving God through the ministry of music. I was encouraged.

The Care of Mom

From a financial perspective, 1969 was not the best year of my life. Having sold the Sunglow Record label, I had no idea what lay ahead for my family and me. My dad's passing left my mother a widow, with two young sons, one just beginning high school and the other in the last year of elementary school. As the oldest in the family, I felt it was appropriate for me to assume responsibility for their well-being.

For a few days, I drove around the neighborhood in a daze, looking for a place that could possibly accommodate my wife and children, as well as my mother and my two youngest siblings. As I drove down a street, about two miles from where Mom lived, I saw a very nice home with a small sign that read, "For Sale by Owners." I thought to myself, *Yeah, right. No money. No credit. Fat chance I have of purchasing that house.* I stopped anyway and rang the doorbell and a very nice woman invited me in to see the house. She spoke to me as though she had known me all of my life. As I shared what had just recently transpired in our life with my dad's passing, she said, "This house would be ideal for you. There is a smaller house in back of the property that could house your mom and your brothers. It is completely furnished, so you would not have to invest in any furniture or appliances." I told her I would check with a mortgage company but my chances would be slim since I didn't have any credit and I had never purchased a home.

Knowing that God promises that He will "supply all of our needs," along with the fact that He cares for and watches after His faithful servants, (i.e., my mother!), I should not have been surprised when the mortgage company approved the loan! We all happily moved into the property shortly thereafter.

Sale of the Sunglow Record Label

After the sale of the Sunglow Records label and the passing of my dad, the Holy Spirit did not fail to provide comfort and assurance that all would well. However, for me and my selfish pride to place all of my trust *completely* in God proved difficult. I started listening to the "doubting, deceitful voice" in my head. It flooded me with thoughts concerning the sale of the record label that included:

> *What if this doesn't work, you will be the laughing-stock of the industry.*
>
> *All that talent you have is just going to go to waste.*
>
> *No one seems to know what they are doing in the industry. It's wide open.*
>
> *Why not start a little record label just to help those people you left stranded? Don't they deserve a chance?*
>
> *You don't have to give up what you are doing if you are happy.*
>
> *You could start a record company in your brother's name. He is still out there."*

My inner struggles continued.

Manny 1969

The Latin Breed Band

In 1970, after close to five years with Sunny, my brother Rudy and several fellow musicians decided to leave Sunny & the Sunliners and start their own group. That was the beginning of The Latin Breed Band, which included vocalist Jimmy Edward.

We immediately started to select and record ten songs for their debut album but found ourselves two songs short to complete a 12-song LP. In the interest of time, I pulled two soundtracks from my archives I had recorded for another artist that were never used. I made a copy for Jimmy to rehearse and two days later, he was ready. He recorded the two songs "Oye Corazon" and "Poquita Fe." The album was a huge success and the two late additions were hits in their own right.

The Latin Breed Band performed at a high level and were genuinely well-received, but gigs were hard to come by and income was so low that the group was forced to disband after a year and a half. At its most difficult juncture, the band traveled to Kingsville, Texas and came away with a grand total of $39, to be equally divided amongst all the band members.

GCP Record Label

Because of my continued inner struggles and doubts, coupled with the fact that my comfort zone was entirely based on the music business I had been a part of for so long, I determined myself to create and establish a new secular record label that ultimately became one of the most successful record labels in the Tejano music industry. I named it "Guerra Company Productions" or "GCP." Before the end of its second year in existence, I had more than twenty-five recording artists under contract. These artists included but were not limited to The Latin Breed, Jimmy Edward, Arturo Montes y Ternura, Roberto Pulido y Los Clasicos, David Marez, Tortilla Factory, and many more.

Hornet's Nest

I continued to enthusiastically attend church and began the studies required to become an ordained minister. I was so grateful to God for all of the wonderful things He was doing in my life. Because of my gratitude, I would volunteer to clean the church and help with anything that needed to be done. As I was working on the church lawn one afternoon, praying as I did so, I told God that I wanted His church to look the best. About that time, I came across a huge tree that was on the side of the church wall. It had long branches that almost reached the ground and had not been trimmed in quite some time. There was a four to five feet tall opening at the bottom of the tree, free from branches. As I pushed the lawn mower into the opening to cut the grass, I began to feel a strange sensation on my back and the pain intensified rapidly. When I pulled the lawn mower out, I saw hundreds of bees. I had disturbed a huge hornet's nest!

Immediately, I turned the lawn mower off and removed my shirt to shake the bees off. The pain was unbearable! I went inside the church, sat on the piano bench and as I leaned onto the piano, I began to cry. It was not the pain from the bee stings that made me cry; I was deeply hurt...with God. I remember asking Him how He could let something like this happen to me, when I was just trying to do the right thing. The moment I questioned God, I felt sunrays coming through a stained-glass window behind me. The heat warmed my back and immediately the pain was gone. It was instantaneous! I drove home and asked my wife to check my back for bee stings; there were none! She said, "There's nothing on your back." "Nothing?" I asked. "Nothing!" she answered. I went into my bedroom, shedding tears of gratitude, thanking the Lord for letting me know He hears me, even in the smallest details of my life.

Having faith in God and walking the road of life with Christ as our Lord and Savior doesn't make Christians immune from the trials, difficulties, and sufferings of life. However, having Christ as Lord of our lives does provide the true believer with spiritual strength to confront the trial, while concurrently providing peace (i.e., joy) that surpasses human understanding as we progress through those trials.

Trusting and resting on the comfort provided by knowing that God is sovereignly in control of all of our life, including our sufferings, enriches, improves, and strengthens our walk with Him. "The righteous person may have many troubles, but the Lord delivers him from them all" (Psalms 34:19).

The Nearness of God

My pastor was a wonderful teacher and became a life-long friend. From the day I received Jesus as my Savior, he would share books that encouraged me in my walk with the Lord. He shared many books on a long-term and continuing basis. My experience has been that filling my mind with information and thoughts about Father God, Jesus Christ, and the Holy Spirit relegates the cares of this world to their appropriate (secondary) status and draws me ever closer to His presence. Many times I felt His divine presence in the dark, quiet, and solitary hours immediately before the dawning of a new day. The Scriptures state that because of His faithfulness, we can "Draw near to God, and He will draw near to you," (James 4:8) and that "God inhabits the praises of His people (Psalms 22:3).

Leading Others to the Saving Grace

In the mid-1970s, the Texas Conference of the denomination I was a member of, assigned me to assist a pastor at a church on the westside of San Antonio. This happened to be the same church where the gentleman who drove across town for my sister and me to attend Sunday school was pastor, sixteen years prior. At that particular point in time, I had been ministering to a person who was very dear to me in the music business. She could see that a change had taken place in my life and wanted to know more about Christianity. After a few months, she decided to submit her life to God and told me she would receive the Lord Jesus Christ as her Savior at the next church service. I prepared a message for the following Sunday.

The day before the Sunday morning service, I came down with a serious stomach virus. I took several over-the-counter medications, but nothing worked. Realizing that I could not possibly stand behind the pulpit in that condition, I drove to my recording studio at 4:00 AM that Sunday morning and recorded the sermon. I had a portable tape recorder and I asked my wife to take it to the pastor and play it on that Sunday morning. At the end of the church service, my friend received the Lord Jesus Christ as her Lord and Savior. Approximately two years later, she led her husband to our Lord Jesus Christ. I was preaching the salvation message that particular Sunday morning as well. He came forward and knelt at the altar. I asked him, "Do you want to receive Jesus Christ as your Lord and Savior?" He responded, "Yes" and added, "...but I am not going to stop drinking." I then said, "I did not ask you that. I asked, 'Do you want to receive Jesus Christ as your Lord and Savior?'" He responded, "Yes." A few years later he became an ordained minister and the pastor of a church. He and his wife became faithful servants of God that led many precious souls to our Lord and Savior, Jesus Christ. To God be the glory in Jesus' name.

The Return of The Latin Breed

In 1971, The Latin Breed Band got together once again and decided to give it another try. We recorded a new LP titled "The Return of The Latin Breed Band," which became one of the biggest selling LPs in Tejano music history. Similar in musical arrangements and wind instrument combinations made popular by mainstream "big bands" like "Chicago" and "Blood, Sweat & Tears," the Latin Breed Band created and established a new standard in the Tejano music industry.

New Recording Equipment

During that time, I applied for a loan at three different banks so I could upgrade my recording studio equipment. All three banks turned me down, which made me eligible to apply for a business loan through the Small Business Administration (SBA); the loan was approved and granted. By 1972, the recording studio was upgraded to near state-of-the-art level. God was continuing to do His work in my life.

Secular Music

For many years, I had the opportunity to meet, interact, work and establish friendships with many talented recording artists and groups. Among many others, these included: Mickey & The Soul Generation, La Mafia, MAZZ, David Marez, Flaco Jimenez, The Royal Jesters, Emilio Navaira, Culturas, Latin Breed Band, Cornelio Reyna, Ramiro Leija & Irene Rivas, Javier Galvan/FAMA, and La Tropa F. But over time, I began to notice that I was starting to feel uneasy about recording secular or "worldly" music. Something inside of me had changed to the point that I no longer wanted to be involved with that type of music. Many of my fellow Christians felt there was nothing wrong with what I was doing. They were so confident in the change God had made in my life, they figured I could not go wrong. Many of them suggested that it was not God who was troubling me about my occupation, but Satan. They went on to explain that Satan knew I could help advance God's work by giving money to establish new churches and he (Satan) did not want that. As a born-again believer, I tried to trust their counsel, but my heart was not convinced. Over time, I noticed that I was gradually recording less and less of the secular music; the desire was no longer there. I shared my conviction with a fellow believer who was also a musician. His response only increased my concern over the topic. He said, "Manny, that is your conviction, not mine. Music is just music. There is no significance either way." Regardless, I could not rationalize the thought that producing secular music, somehow, glorified God.

I never believed playing or listening to secular music was sinful, until I learned from studying Scripture that Lucifer was the "master-musician" who led praise and worship to God Himself. Learning this made me wonder:

> *When Lucifer was cast down to earth from heaven, would he not use his 'musical gifts and talents' to deceive unsuspecting followers and would-be followers of Jesus Christ?*
>
> *Would not the premise of "garbage in, garbage out" apply here?*

I discussed this subject with a pastor that I trusted. He simply said, "You have become legalistic," which was something I did not expect or want to hear. Immediately after speaking with the pastor, I realized Satan was behind all the contradictory and persuasive invading my mind:

> *Don't be a fool, don't stop doing what you are doing.*
> *God wants you to make a lot of money to help build new churches where many souls will be saved.*
> *Don't mess up a good thing.*
> *Look at how God is blessing you with new business.*
> *The more successful you are, the more you can help support the Lord's work. Don't mess it up now.*

It didn't take me long to come to the realization that God didn't need "*my money*," which was His all along, anyway; something that my self-centered view did not see or comprehend at the time. Looking back, knowing what I know now, I was correct in my thinking that my efforts to develop and produce secular music were, in fact, not pleasing or glorifying to God. But instead of having enough conviction and determination to make a clean break from it and because of my lack of trust and faith to totally depend on Him, I allowed and actually *used* other people's thoughts and opinions to sway me and stop me from doing what the conviction of my heart told me was right and wrong.

God's Involvement in Our Daily Lives

There were multiple instances when extraordinary and unexplainable occurrences took place in the recording studio. One occasion in particular was when I had a well-known group coming in for their first recording session at my studio. I was setting up the 2" recording tape on the 24-track tape recorder and the machine would not play. I didn't know what to do. Usually when something was malfunctioning on the recorder, it would cost $500 for airfare to fly a technician in, which was in addition to the actual costs of parts and repair. In this particular instance, the problem was not the cost; it was that I needed an immediate remedy, in time for the recording session scheduled to begin within the hour. At that point, I did the only thing I could do. I appealed to God! I prayed, "Please help me Lord, I am really in a tight spot here."

There was a panel right under the deck on the recorder. I clicked it open and thought to myself, *"What are you going to do now, you don't know anything about the workings of this machine."* As I sat in front of the open panel, I found myself staring at an outrageous number of wires intricately connected throughout the entire circuit board; I was searching for a needle in a haystack. Within seconds, my eyes focused on one very small wire, which seemed to be disconnected from the circuit board. I inserted it…and the machine was fixed!

Some will say it was "a coincidence" and that "it's so minor, you shouldn't even have mentioned it." I will say it was the kindness of a gracious God, who has an interest and cares, even about the details of our every-day lives. "Give *all* your worries and cares to God, for He cares about you" (1 Peter 5:7).

An Obscene Telephone Call

One night, I was startled and awakened by a telephone call. It was just past midnight. When I answered, the voice on the other end sounded like what I would have imagined Satan's raspy and harsh voice would sound like. As I heard the demonic voice speak, it sent chills down my spine. My first reaction was to hang up, but something told me that was too easy. I prayed, *Lord, what would you have me do in a situation like this? Why did you permit such a call to reach me?* I was reminded that God cared about the person on the other end of the phone. As I kept hearing the obscenities on the other end of the telephone, I wondered if the *moment I tell him Jesus loves him, he is going to hang up.* I waited for an opening, then I said, "Jesus loves you."

There was silence…and I repeated, "Jesus loves you."

The sound of the caller's voice changed and he asked, "What did you say?"

I repeated, "Jesus loves you."

The voice asked, "Why did you say that?"

"Because He does."

Then he said, "Are you a brother?"

"Yes, I am a believer and I serve the Lord Jesus Christ."

He replied, "You do?"

"Yes, I do."

Then he said, "You mean, after all those things I said, He still loves me?"

"Yes, He does! That's why He permitted you to call this number. Do you want me to tell you about Jesus?"

"Yes," the voice answered.

"I want to tell you about him but there is something you must do first."

"What?" he asked.

I said, "You must show me that you are sincere about wanting to know about Jesus by giving me your phone number, so that I can call you back. This way I will know you really mean it."

"No!" was the quick reply. "You will report me!"

I assured him that I would not.

After a little more talking, he agreed and gave me the number. I said, "I will call you right back."

I did...and to my surprise, it was a young girl. I was able to share the Lord Jesus Christ with her. I rejoiced in the Lord for yet another experience He allowed me to have. Any other time in my life, I would simply have hung the phone up from the start.

God's Mercy in the Dominican Republic

In 1972, I was invited to attend a Latin Fellowship Minister's Conference in Santo Domingo in the Dominican Republic. The location where the conference was to be held was called "Jarabacoa," which was on a mountain, approximately 60 miles from Santo Domingo. It had a hotel sitting at the top of the mountain and nothing else. The entire hotel had been reserved for the convergence of delegates from many countries, including Brazil, Haiti, Mexico,

Central America, and the United States. I was fortunate enough to go as an honorary delegate from Texas. Additionally, I had the opportunity to meet with the pastor of the church on the westside of San Antonio, who was the same gentle soul who would drive across town every Sunday to bring my sister and me to Sunday school. It was a wonderful Spirit-filled four days. God greatly moved among the ministers, including a bishop, as we all united in prayer and worship.

The morning after the fellowship had adjourned, we were each to check a bulletin board to see which specifically-assigned car would be taking each of us down from the mountain and back to Santo Domingo. I remember seeing my name assigned to the same Dominican couple I had ridden with up the mountain. However, a few minutes later, as I re-checked the bulletin board, I noticed that I had been reassigned to ride in a different vehicle. Apparently, when the Dominican couple heard about or saw the change in assigned vehicles, they went to the person in charge and convinced him to assign me back to their vehicle. Those riding in the vehicle were the Dominican couple, a bishop, a newspaper reporter for the denomination, a brother from California, and me. At the appropriate time, we departed for the steep return trip down the mountain.

As we traveled, we discussed the great outpouring of the Holy Spirit and the other wonderful things that had been shared during the conference. After a few minutes, an emotional reaction from the driver's wife interrupted our conversation. As the vehicle continued to pick up speed, she kept telling her husband to slow down and not to drive down the mountain road so fast. The smell of something burning filled the vehicle. I was seated on the passenger-side front seat and the driver's wife was seated in the middle seat. As I glanced at the driver, I noticed that he was starting to panic and his wife had started to cry. The driver, inexperienced in driving in the mountainous terrain, had been driving with his foot on the brake pedal (i.e., "riding the brakes"), which caused the brakes to overheat and lock-up. At that point, the mountain was so steep that we could not see the bottom of the cliff. The shoulder of the road extended two or three feet to my right, with no guardrail that might keep us from going over the side. To our left was the side of the mountain, with huge boulders and oncoming traffic.

As different scenarios raced through my mind, the idea that seemed easiest and most prudent for my own personal benefit was for me to jump out of the vehicle. As I reached for the door handle, my thoughts and concerns returned to the others in the station wagon. Looking back on the experience, I am convinced that only Divine Intervention could have made me overcome the selfish desire to save myself. I quickly reached across the driver's wife, grabbed the steering wheel and jerked it toward the mountainside, chancing a head-on collision. The station wagon hit and came to a sudden but safe stop against a boulder.

As we all got out of the vehicle, I decided I would walk the rest of the way down the mountain. However, the other passengers all convinced me I could not do that without risking being struck by oncoming vehicular traffic. The brother from California said he had experience driving over mountainous terrain, so we waited for the brakes to cool down, he took the wheel and drove the rest of the way. Once we reached the bottom of the mountain, I recall telling the bishop, "Sir, you were the only one who didn't panic." He replied, "It is just that I am older and it takes me a little bit longer to react." Of course, I knew that was not the entire reason. He was calm simply because he was confident that if he had lost his earthly life that day, he would instantly open his spiritual and eternal eyes to see Jesus Christ face-to-face. God, in His sovereignty and providence had, once again, demonstrated His supernatural power of love, grace, and mercy.

Falling Away

Back home, all seemed to be going well with me in the church… or so I thought. Satan, with all his cunning, had set it up perfectly for me. I was experiencing blessings and fulfillment as I consistently attended church. I was preaching as a layperson and was progressing toward ordination. Sunday school attendance was up and other events and activities encouraged people to attend church. There was nothing I could not handle…or so I thought. "Therefore, let him who thinks he stands take heed lest he fall" (1 Corinthians 10:12). Before I realized it, I had turned loose of God's guiding hand and had given in to temptation and fallen into the pit of sin that Jesus had rescued me from. "But each person is tempted when he is carried away and enticed by his own lust (desires). Then when lust has conceived, it gives birth to sin..." (James 1:14-15). The Bible teaches that "For out of the heart come evil thoughts...adulteries...sexual immoralities..." (Matthew 15:19). I took my eyes off of God, I fell, and I had absolutely no one to blame but myself. Further compounding the situation, devious thoughts entered my mind:

> *You don't need to tell anyone. It will destroy your testimony.*
> *Maybe you were not even "born again" to begin with.*
> *Maybe your mother brainwashed you and you got carried away with your emotions.*

I countered with:

> *I really am saved and my life has changed. This is not a put-on."*

But my contrary thoughts continued:

> *How could you say you were saved from sin and of what God did for you and then you turn right around and sin?*
> *How can you be telling others that God delivers from sin and you are still caught up in it?*

My sinful mind *was* able to convince me that it was all a lie and that I was a liar:

> *You aren't any good. You're a con artist. I knew it from the beginning. You are just a show-off— wherever you are, you have to be in the spotlight.*
> *You were optimistic about becoming an ordained minister. You thought that you would be*

a leader in the church. You were always only seeking
what you wanted.

Well, Mr. Know-It-All, the best thing you can
do now is leave the church before you contaminate
them all.

I fell for the sinful and rebellious thoughts. I was discouraged and unable to talk about it with anyone. I did not dare go to the pastor; it would have disappointed him. I could not go to Mom; it would surely have broken her heart. I was confused and alone. It seemed that God was a million miles away. Scripture states that God promises "No temptation has overtaken you that is not common to man; and God is faithful, and He will not let you be tempted beyond your ability, but with the temptation He will also provide the way of escape, that you may be able to endure it." (Corinthians 10:13). That promise remains as true and as powerful as ever but in order for God to do His work, we *must* humble ourselves and give ourselves over to His leading. We must diligently seek Him, setting our own selfish interests and thoughts aside. My failure occurred and, in fact, worsened because I took matters into my own hands. I did not step aside and let God do His work. Instead, I seized the reins of control, using my own limited, wayward, and sinful reasoning, ignoring the guidance that God faithfully provided through His Word.

My sinful nature continued to bombard me:

Well, does that not say it all? Did you not give
in to temptation and fall into sin? Does that not
prove that you are not a child of God? If you were,
He would not have let this happen to you. Why don't
you just give this whole thing up? It doesn't work!

In the weeks that followed, I tried to confess my sins at the altar but doubting thoughts from the father of lies did not cease:

What about those people who have been saved
because of your testimony? What are they going

to think? They are going to think that God really does not have the power to help them with their sin problem.

You are actually thinking of confessing to the whole church—after all the things you have taught them? What a dark day it will be when the whole church knows that one of its leaders has fallen into sin. It will certainly kill many Christians, spiritually."

My sinful mind also succeeded in making me believe God could not be trusted:

God let you down after all you have done for Him.
After leaving your business, after giving so much to His work and this is the way He treats you."

Ironically, all of the miracles that God had graced me with were never recalled. I completely forgot or overlooked all the instances when God had, in fact, seen me through.

I tried to continue preaching, but I couldn't. I felt like the Spirit of God had left me. Obviously, He had not left me; it was me who had rejected and distanced myself from Him. I was on the verge of confessing my sin from the pulpit. I wanted to say, "I'm sorry, I've sinned against God and against you, please forgive me" but my depraved mind and sinful heart caused fear to hold me back. I did not stand a chance. It was not long after that I quit preaching the Word of God. I made excuses for not taking an active part in church and soon I stopped going to church altogether.

Rebellion

To that point in time, I believed I had been saved or born again, by the grace of God on June 2, 1968 but after four years, I became so bitter, prideful, and selfish that I began lashing out at the people who called themselves Christians. Instead of looking inwardly for the source of the problem, which is where the *real problem* was, I turned all of my bitterness toward others, particularly believers. I became hateful and jealous of those who were serving God. I found fault in everyone...except myself. My bruised pride and my refusal to take responsibility for my own failures caused me to divert the focus away from me and project my disappointment and shortcomings onto others. I remember arrogantly telling God, "If these are the people you are taking to heaven and I will have to live with for eternity, then I pass!" I discouraged anyone who tried to witness to me. I went to the unreasonable and blasphemous extreme of telling them there was no God! That it was all in their heads. Going forward, I planned to completely rely on myself; no help needed! This time I was not going to listen to anyone, especially those who served God. Strategically, I was going to build a wall of work and debt big enough and thick enough to keep me busy and focused, while at the same time, making myself as inaccessible to God as possible. Instead of humbling myself before Holy God, admitting my sinfulness, mourning my waywardness, and pleading for forgiveness, my prideful, sinful nature led me to the other extreme, angrily and foolishly entrenching myself against Almighty God.

Back to Playing in a Band

In 1973, with the thought that being out among the people again would do me some good, I began to frequent a small, neighborhood club in northwest San Antonio where a group of friends performed. As I listened to the music on a regular basis, it wasn't long before I felt the urge to play drums again. Shortly thereafter, I learned their drummer was leaving and before I could give it a second thought, I had the drummer's job. I played with the group for a few weeks but quickly realized the band had no real leadership. We all talked it over and soon I was managing the band. We got serious about our work and before long, the club was frequently packed to capacity. I started drinking again, except now I was drinking heavily. For the first time in my life, at the age of 35, I experimented with marijuana. My life was so empty that oftentimes I wished the hours at the club would never end. I knew that away from the busyness of the club, I would find myself alone…just thinking. I had a wife and children at home, but I wanted to keep my problems away from them, which ironically, only caused more problems for them.

My experience with marijuana was short-lived. It was during the fifteen-minute breaks between sets at the club that I started to join the other members of the group in smoking. One night, what we smoked may have been laced with some other substance because, while I remembered getting home at close to 2:00 AM, I don't remember how I got there. All I remember is that one moment I was leaving the club and in the next moment, I was in the den of my home, which was 12 miles away. I asked my wife to cook breakfast for me and while I was waiting, I decided to watch TV. After a few minutes, my wife asked, "What are you doing?" I said, "I'm watching television. She said, "There's no TV at this hour, it's past midnight; they're signed off the air. There's nothing but snow on the screen!"

As she walked back to the kitchen, I began to feel like I couldn't breathe. I felt like I was about to suffocate. As I attempted to gasp for air, somehow, I was able to generate a scream to my wife. She ran over to me and asked, "What's wrong!?" I kept telling her, "I can't breathe, I'm going to die!" She noticed that I was trying to gasp for air through my nose, so she instructed me to open my mouth to breathe. Only then did I realize that the weed I had smoked had apparently stopped-up my nose. It was one of the most horrifying moments of my life. Needless to say, that was the last time I ever smoked marijuana.

A Consistent Calling from God

Although I would ignore Him and not respond, God never stopped reaching for me. He spoke to me in various ways, at different times. I knew He was speaking but I was still arrogantly angry with Him for erroneously thinking He had not protected me from falling and for allowing people from the church to lash out at me and hurt me. I resolved I did not want Him or His help. One thing I noticed was that no matter where I was, I found myself consistently bringing up and talking to people about the things of God. Can you imagine how ridiculous that was; sitting there half-drunk, "preaching" to whomever would listen.

During those dark days, there was only one person who consistently came around to check on me. Over the years, I had befriended a drunkard who roamed the streets in and around the recording studio. He would knock on my studio door, open it, and say "Manuelito, I don't want to take up too much of your time. I just want to tell you that the Lord loves you and so do I." He would then close the door and be gone as quickly as he had appeared.

My Brother's New Life In Christ

In 1974, my younger brother Rudy received Jesus Christ as his Lord and Savior and *completely* surrendered his life to God. Shortly thereafter, He advised fellow Latin Breed members that he would stay with the band for one year in order to fulfill all their commitments but that he would be leaving the band after the year was completed.

The Birthday Gift

As mentioned, there were numerous times during those dark days in my life that God made His presence known. One such instance was during my thirty-fifth birthday celebration. Many of my friends filled the club for the celebration. Even though it was a weekday, the place was packed. Midway through the celebration, as I opened gifts friends had given me, there was a dimming of the lights and a lot of commotion at the entrance to the club. I could not make it out, but I knew my friends were up to something. As my nickname ("La Borrega") was announced over the sound system, I was asked to come to the stage. I made my way up to the platform where two of my buddies were waiting for me. I asked them what was going on. The lights came on and the whole crowd shouted, "Happy Birthday, Borrega!" and there, at the center of the dance floor, was a live baby lamb. The yelling of the crowd noise scared it, causing it to fall to its knees. While people were laughing, my heart sank. I immediately recalled scripture that stated: "Behold, the Lamb of God, who takes away the sins of the world" (John 1:29). As I began to breakdown, I asked God, "How can you hurt me like this?" He spoke to my heart and said, "Just as you see how absolutely out of place this lamb is, you too are out of place here. This is not where you belong." I took the lamb in my arms, went outside, and wept uncontrollably. *Nothing* is more powerful than the love of God.

Living Alone

Living my selfish lifestyle, obviously with *me* at the center of it, soon took its toll on my home life. Soon, I found an apartment, moved out of the house, and tried living alone. Before long, I was bored with everything I did. I spent long hours watching television. When I got tired of that, I started the movie theater bit, then tried going to different clubs. It seems I always ended up at the club where I performed on the weekends. I never saw any members of the band there during the week; it was just a weekend job for them and they had their own private lives to tend to.

Special Messenger

One weekday, while at the club, I purchased a drink at the bar and returned to the back room where the pool tables were located. At that moment, I sensed an awareness that I had previously only experienced with the things of God. All of a sudden, the drink did not taste good anymore. As I tried to concentrate on the pool game, the person with me sensed that something was up and asked, "What's wrong?" I did not answer. As I tried to get back to the game, I heard voices of people entering the club. It was one of the musicians I worked with on the weekends. He was introducing someone to the club owner, then he turned and saw me from afar and said, "Just the man I wanted to see. I *knew* I would find you here." He came to where I was and said, "There is someone I want you to meet." I walked over to the gentleman he was referring to and I shook his hand, as my friend said, "Manny, I want you to meet a good friend of mine. We were in the Army together and we have not seen each other in over twenty-five years." My friend asked if I had a few minutes so we could go into the other room and talk. I handed the cue stick to the person I was with, picked up my drink, and followed them into the next room.

As we sat down, my friend told me a strange thing had happened that I should know about. He said, "I will let my friend explain. Maybe you guys can figure it out." His friend said, "I had not seen my buddy here since we were discharged from the Army over twenty years ago. After our time in the Army, we never saw each other again. I was explaining to him that I own a steel manufacturing plant in Detroit and I spend a lot of time traveling to Full Gospel men's meetings. I found the Lord some years ago, so every chance I have, I travel to different cities sharing my story (testimony). I was changing planes in Dallas, headed to Houston and somehow I boarded the wrong plane and ended up here in San Antonio. I remembered my old Army buddy, so I looked through the telephone directory but did not find his name listed. I assumed, after all this time, he had probably moved away. The Spirit led me to call Information and the operator gave me his number. To my friend here, all of this is a strange coincidence, but I know better. After telling him what had transpired, he asked me how I found his telephone number. I told him that the Operator had given it to me. Then he said, 'That's impossible! My number is private; it's not listed!' When I told him about my spiritual life, he said, 'What a coincidence, we have a drummer in our group that used to be a preacher too.' I asked him if he could take me to him and here we are. I just want to give you this message and I will be going. God loves you so much that He wants me to share with you that you have hurt and punished yourself long enough. You need to come back to Him, where you belong. Right now, He is keeping a few hundred men in Houston waiting, so He could divert me to San Antonio, so I could deliver this message to you, *personally*." He said, "May God bless you" and just like that, he was gone.

I was encouraged! I called my wife to tell her what had happened and that I needed to talk with her. I went home that night and as my wife and children all surrounded me, we wept until there were no more tears. My wife and I decided to give it another try. We had already filed for a divorce, so a few weeks after it became final, we were remarried.

History Repeats Itself

We started to attend church regularly, but the initial feelings of the joy of my salvation were gone. I struggled to stay in church and I said, "Lord, even if I do not feel anything, I know you're real; I'm going to serve you by faith." I prayed but my prayers did not seem to go past the ceiling. I was feeling like a hypocrite. In my prayers, I was saying, "God, I know you called me back but what is happening to me? Why can't I sense your presence?" My sin-prone heart instigated doubting and disturbing messages yet again. Again, the seeds of doubt began to sprout:

> *This is as good as it's going to get for you. This is all you can expect from God. He gave you His Holy Spirit once, but you lost Him.*
>
> *You didn't really think you could just change your mind and come back, did you?*
>
> *It was not God who called you back, you were just coming to the end of your rope and since you couldn't hack it anymore, you made yourself think that God wanted you back; wishful thinking on your part.*
>
> *You do not belong to God.*
>
> *His people cannot trust you anymore. Can't you see how they are afraid to associate with you in church?*
>
> *You let God down so many times and you will do it again. You cannot be trusted.*
>
> *You live in sin and as soon as your conscience convicts you, you want to come back to God. That's not going to work. You should get a hold of yourself and stop playing the church game.*
>
> *Get to taking care of your recording business before you lose it all. That's all you have left."*

I waited to see if God would somehow counter; if He would give me some sort of sign...but there was nothing. I started to turn loose of His guiding hand yet again. Once again, I buried myself in my work and spent all my time working. That was the only way I would not think about the things of God. The business increased its revenues, but I stopped giving to the church. I thought that if God did not want me, I figured He didn't want anything to do with my dirty money either. I was not going to be giving money to a church that I thought didn't care about me.

Lady On A Plane Flight

I started drinking again. One day, as I was returning home from a business trip to Dallas, I was sitting next to an elderly woman on the plane. I had quite a few drinks at the airport and was ordering more drinks on the plane. Intoxicated as I was, I started a conversation with her. As we talked, she mentioned the Lord. I asked her if she was a Christian and she answered, "Yes, I am." I shared about the many wonderful things God had done in my life. I admitted to her, as if it wasn't obvious, that I was a backslider and had fallen away.

Near the end of the forty-five-minute flight, we stopped talking for a few minutes. She then turned to me and said, "I don't understand how anyone who is backslidden could be such a blessing." I was quick to answer that it was not anything I had done. God loved her so much He was willing to use a drunkard to tell her that. As we were leaving the plane, she smiled and said, "I will be praying for you. I am confident you will be alright with God." She added, "Don't punish yourself so much, Manny." With that she walked off. Other passengers who had apparently overheard our conversation, gave their smile of approval as well.

Success with GCP Label

In 1975, at one of the industry's award events, GCP walked away with eight of the ten awards, including Record Company of the Year. But soon, just like before, success in the recording industry was not enough for me, so I began searching elsewhere. I was bored and continued to crave whatever it was that could fill the void in my life.

Little did I know that before the year ended, boredom would be the very least of my worries.

Emotional and Personal Turmoil

In the summer of 1975, as I was starting a recording session, I felt a heavy feeling of depression come over me. The only way I can describe it was what I thought it would feel like to fall off a cliff, with the inability to stop or help myself. I was terrified and I started to panic. I had never experienced anything like that before. I waited for it to pass but it only got worse. I stood up and as I left the group of musicians I was recording, I signaled to an employee to come to the other room.

"I've got to get out of here," I said.

"What's wrong, Manny?"

I don't know," I answered, "but I've got to leave!"

As I drove home, it felt as if I was losing my mind. I ran into the house and went straight to the bedroom. My wife asked, "What's wrong with you? You're as white as a sheet!" I told her I did not know what was happening to me but to please bring the children to me. While she gathered them, I remember changing into my pajamas and crawling into bed, covering myself with the covers. All I could think of doing was to pray. As the children came in, I asked them to please pray for me because something was happening to their daddy that I had no control over and I needed their prayers. They prayed and hugged me as hard as they could. All four were around me, asking, "What's wrong, Daddy?" I kept repeating, "I don't know. I need you all very close to me right now." After a few minutes, the horrible feeling passed. To this day, I have never been able to precisely describe the panic I went through. The experience helped me realize that the fear of losing your mind is, likely, the most horrible experience anyone could ever have. As I shared this experience with close friends, some of them said I was working too many hours without rest. Others said it was my drinking. One person said, "I've seen this happen to someone before. You had the symptoms of a nervous breakdown." Whatever it was, I slowed the pace down considerably

79

at work and continually hoped that type of experience would never reoccur to me or anyone else I cared about.

I felt like a total failure. I did not want to live anymore but I was afraid to die. Every time I thought of death, I felt as helpless as a child. At that point, I no longer waited for the evening hours to pour myself a drink. I was shortening the workday and sending my employee out for a bottle of Scotch. The alcohol was taking me to a place where there was no pain and no worry; nothing but laughter. I remember asking my friends, "Could I have become an alcoholic?" They would say, "No way, man! You just like to have fun." In hindsight, I was clearly a drunkard.

Soon the trouble extended to my family. I began to threaten my wife. She feared that one day I would come in drunk and physically hurt her. It was difficult seeing what I was putting my family through. "This is not going to work," I said, "I want a divorce." Without hesitation, she responded with, "That's fine with me." So, my wife and I went through a 2nd divorce. After such a bright beginning, I certainly never thought it would turn out like it did.

After the divorce, I rented an apartment and I continued drinking heavily. When I was left to myself, I was very lonely. I had always thought that being single was the way to go, but the single life was turning out to be a very lonely place for me. I was vulnerable. I remember talking to God once again and saying, "Look down on me and see what a mess I have made of my life and the lives of others." I continued to ask Him to help me. He never turned away from me as I continued to confess my sins and seek His mercy. Slowly but surely, He created a desire in my heart to draw near to Him. I tried to go back where I thought I had left Him...in church, but my spirit was more oppressed as I forced myself to attend church services. Familiar doubting and negative thoughts harassed me:

You haven't received your just punishment yet!
You can't expect God to take you back, just like that.

Young Lady

In 1977, I met a young lady who was halfway through college, majoring in media broadcasting. She was working at a radio station on weekends and was interested in Tejano music. I accompanied our record promoter to dinner with her. We talked about the music business, which seemed to provide us a forum for interesting conversations. One thing led to another and a few months later, we were married. I thought to myself, "*This is what I needed, a wife who can be involved with me in the business. We actually have something in common.*" I shared my past spiritual experiences and continued to share the Lord Jesus Christ with her. We started attending church and soon, through our Bible studies at home, she gave her heart to the Lord. Everything seemed to be okay now.

The Baptism

For several months, my wife and I attended a church where my mother had been temporarily assigned as pastor. As I was praying, I was prompted to assess my personal history regarding baptism. As a child, I had been baptized in a Catholic church and to this point had felt it was enough. However, now I felt it would be pleasing to God for me to be baptized by submersion. As I continued to pray, my thoughts came to rest on a particular minister who could perform the baptism, but I felt a certain reluctance to reach out to him, knowing he was well aware of my failings related to the Christian walk. Besides, the likelihood of having this particular gentleman involved was remote, since I had not seen him for quite a few years. Regardless, I prayed about it and left it in God's hands.

Two days later, as my wife and I were eating lunch at a local restaurant, I was shocked when I looked out the window and saw the particular minister in question...walking into the restaurant! As soon as I saw him, I immediately knew that God had sovereignly caused our paths to cross. While I initially remained reluctant to approach him, by the time the minister had seen me and made his way to our table, the Lord had softened my stance and strengthened me to ask him for his forgiveness and to request his assistance in my baptism.

Within a few days, we met at the river behind Mission County Park. The river ran deep at this location. Frankly, I had never seen the San Antonio River as full as it was that day. The minister, my wife, and my mother were the only witnesses to the event. The minister went into the water and I followed, while my wife and mother stayed by the river's edge. It was a clear and beautiful sunny day. As the minister put me under water, I heard a loud thunderous noise. I thought it was the water splashing up against my ears as I went under. The minister raised me up from the water and I could hear him loudly praising the Lord. There had been loud clap of thunder, then it had started to rain! My wife and mother began to weep. I knew that this experience was the result of my obedience to God. He was once again confirming His presence in my life. The moment the minister and I stepped out of the water, the rain stopped and the sun continued to shine. After such an event, I figured nothing could ever defeat me again. Surely, this was an indication that God was going to handle everything from now on. Satan would not be able to trap me again.

The IRS

My wife worked hard to help me keep the business going. During the second year of our marriage, the Internal Revenue Service (IRS) conducted an audit on our business, going back three years. While I thought we would be fine, they did find some discrepancies on my returns. It seemed that my bookkeeper was deducting all items purchased during the year at full cost, instead of putting them on a depreciation list. Now with penalties and interests, I owed the IRS twenty thousand dollars and it was due immediately. I met with an IRS representative and asked if I could pay it in installments. She responded, "We are not a loan institution, Mr. Guerra. Why don't you borrow it from your bank? Your full payment will be due within thirty days."

It was like the end of the world for me. I was forced to sell the GCP Company. That meant I would have to start all over again. The IRS allowed us some time to find a buyer. Ironically, the buyer turned out to be the same person who had talked Sunny Ozuna into leaving the Sunglows back in 1964. We sold the company and were left with the equipment debt to SBA and another banking institution. I discussed my situation with my attorney and asked him what he thought I should do. He said, "The best thing for you to do is file for bankruptcy. You will never get out of this one."

The first transaction I made after the sale of the GCP Records label was to write a check for the full amount I owed my special friend, (the grocery store owner). I handed him a check for $24,000 and said, "This is the God that I now serve and the God who loves you." He sat there, stunned. He could not believe what had just happened.

Divorced Again

I continued working in the studio day and night. It was not long before the influences of the world attacked my weakness and contaminated me yet again. The groups I was recording were with big record labels and soon, I was contracted to produce all of their music. They brought in all kinds of drugs but thankfully, I was not into that. The weapon of choice for the devil to use to initiate my downfalls was always marital unfaithfulness. By the time I realized it, I was sinking into sin yet again. I felt that if I had an ounce of decency left in me, I would let my wife go back to her hometown and give her a chance to make a life for herself. She was still young and she certainly didn't deserve this. I informed her that I knew that I could never be the kind of husband she deserved and I asked her to go back home. Against her wishes and protests, I sent her home. After five years of marriage, I was alone once more and I vowed never to marry again, as I continued to bury myself in my work.

New Record Label

In 1982, I established yet another record label and named it "Record Producer" or "RP Records and Tapes." My intent for the new label was to help the newer, younger artists who were predominately ignored in the music business. It was apparent to me that no one wanted to help these "newcomer" groups who were not yet known in the industry. I had a sense of compassion for them, having known and remembered the headaches and heartaches I had personally endured while trying to break into the music business. Among those unknown groups was a family band out of Corpus Christi known as "Selena y Los Dinos."

The father, whom I had known for several years and who also doubled as the band's manager, called and asked if I could produce an album for his kids. Over the next three years, I produced four long-play (LP) albums for the group. The first three did not sell well but the fourth album sold more than the first three combined. With some extra promotion, Selena won the "Best Female Artist of the year" at the Tejano Music Awards (in San Antonio) and went on to a hugely successful career, crossing genres along the way.

Another Chance

Contrary to my vow of not marrying again, in 1987, I married a widowed woman and I continued to slowly but surely chip away at my business debts. After we were married, things started to go better for me in general and in 1990, I established the "Manny Music" record label. I finalized a record deal with Sony Discos (CBS-owned) to distribute our product, which proved to be a good move for my business.

Motivated from an Unexpected Source

During 1988 and mainly because of poor business practices, I struggled to stay in business. Needless to say, I was feeling down. About that time, an insurance agent/friend had stopped by the studio. As I shared all that was happening, he stood across my recording mixing console and said, "Manny, I've known you all your life. I remember when you started out. Many people thought you would fold within a short time. You had a dream and that dream built several successful music companies. You have played a major part in the creation and development of the Tejano music industry. You always told me how God helped you build all of this. He doesn't want it to go down the drain." Although this gentleman never professed to be a believer, he was encouraging me to trust God. "If you did it once, you can do it again," he confidently stated. I was very encouraged. I knew I only had enough money to make payments for the next two months, so I scheduled a meeting with representatives from the Small Business Administration (SBA). They reviewed my files and said, "We will help you by deferring or postponing payments for one year. After that, we'll see what it looks like and if it looks good, we will try to cut your monthly payments in half." I asked, "Do you think the loan institution will give me the same break?" "That's up to them," they said. "If they decide to foreclose, they will have to come to us because we have first lien on everything you own."

After that, I went to the Savings & Loan and met with the loan officer who had helped me get established. I explained my situation and told him about the break SBA had given me. He said, "We cannot defer payments, but I'll go to bat for you and try to get the loan committee to cut your payments in half." He called me after a week and said I could come in and sign documents. "What documents?" I asked. He said, "We are going to refinance your note because the interest rate is much lower now than when you borrowed the money. Someone must be looking out for you." I cancelled all my credit cards and wrote them a letter of apology. I told them it would take a little time but I promised to pay each and every one of them back. It took ten years…but I paid them all in full!

With the good news of the second chance my lenders had granted me came the realization that I had become a workaholic. All I thought about was getting out of debt. I became very difficult to get along with during those days. Instead of seeing God's mercies, the enemy kept reminding me that if I had not wasted my money over the years, I would not be in this mess. Satan fooled me into digging myself deeper and deeper into a hole, creating an obstacle between God and me.

Mom's Dream

One day, while my brother Rudy visited me at the studio and we shared some of the experiences we had in the Lord, I told him that it seemed as if producing secular music kept me from serving God. He quickly replied, "Has Mom ever told you of the dream she had about you concerning music?"

"No" I said, "When did this happen?"

"It was quite a while ago. I guess she didn't share it because you weren't serving the Lord," He said.

"What's it about?" I asked.

He said, "You better let Mom tell you; I may miss some of the details."

I called Mom and asked her about her dream. She explained that she had this dream during the mid-70s.

I asked, "Why didn't you ever tell me?"

She said, "I tried but you weren't interested."

"Well, I'm interested now!"

She had this dream just before I backslid the first time. She said I was lying on the ground and my wife was kneeling over my body. When Mom saw me on the ground, she ran toward me. She asked my wife what had happened. My wife answered, "He's half dead" and she pointed toward the giant who was fleeing the scene. She informed Mom that the giant had done this. "That giant left him half dead!" she said. When Mom saw the giant, she began to pursue him with a rod in her hands. As Mom chased the giant, a sister in Christ attempted to tell her that the giant was the same one that had injured her own son, but Mom continued giving chase and told the sister, "I'll talk with you later."

She caught up with the giant and started to beat him with the rod. Her aim was for his head but she was unable to hit her mark because the giant kept moving to avoid her blows. However, after a while and apparently exhausted from the hits that Mom *had* managed to land, the giant got up and retreated to his dwelling, which was an underground cave. At this point, Mom continued to chase him. As the giant entered his dwelling, he left the door slightly open and Mom could see that he was exhausted and was trying desperately to catch his breath. He leaned against an enormous computer-like recording console and his hands were moving quickly on the mixing board. He turned on a switch that caused loud, boisterous music to play. As he listened to the music, his strength and size began to increase, as if instant energy were being pumped into him. It seemed that with every musically-filled breath he took, he got stronger and his size continued to expand.

As he continued to listen to the power-generating music, a sudden interference, similar to when two radio signals or frequencies try to merge into one, was heard. The voice that was filtering through was that of a man preaching the Gospel of Jesus Christ. As the voice of the preacher with the heavenly message reached the giant's hearing, he became very distressed and very troubled and began to quiver and shrink and shrivel up, as fear decreased his strength. At that point, the giant started to chew on his fingernails, shaking, and becoming very agitated and uneasy. As the loud music increased, the giant's strength increased in proportion. At a particular point, the preacher's voice again filtered through the noise and the giant again weakened. According to Mom, the messenger's voice was dominant and audible on three distinct occasions and each time the message filtered through, the phrase "*the blood of Jesus Christ*" was heard.

As Mom continued to observe, she saw how the giant became strong and how he became weak. At the time he received the last surge of power from the music, he turned and saw Mom looking through the open door. The giant became furious and rushed to attack her. As he advanced toward her, Mom again took hold of the rod and shouted "In the name of Jesus!" and "Through the blood of Jesus!" and the giant held back and became powerless. With every attempt he made to attack her, she repeated the same verbiage and each time, the giant would back off. At one point, Mom noticed that the giant was headed for me and she proceeded to try to stop him. As Mom and the giant came close to where I was lying, a sister in Christ ran to meet her. As she tried to explain about the giant, Mom quickly answered that she knew who he was now and that she knew he was causing destruction in her son's life. The giant then changed his course of direction and turned away from me. Mom came back to where I was and asked my wife how I was doing. She answered, "He seems to be coming around."

Mom didn't know who or what the giant was or represented until the day she was watching me being interviewed on television. I was asked what I thought about Tejano music and my response was, "Tejano music is a sleeping giant that is about to wake up." *Immediately,* the Spirit of God revealed the identity of the menacing giant in her dream.

Embarrassing, Painful Moment

One day, there was a faint knock at the door of my recording studio. I said, "Come in." It was a very dear friend whom I had not seen for quite some time. Through the partially opened door, he jokingly but profoundly asked, "I just wanted to check; should I come in with a bottle of Scotch or a Bible?" In summary, that is how my erratic and extreme Christian walk had transpired. My friend thought it was funny, but God used him to make me realize how others viewed my inconsistencies and variances and how contrary and contradictory my testimony had been perceived. A testimony that had, no doubt, caused confusion, uncertainties, hesitancy, skepticism and mistrust of the Christian walk by those who witnessed it...and I had only myself to blame for that.

Studio Dreaming

In 1987, I decided to start making plans for a new recording studio I would build if I was ever financially able to do so. I not only started to draw plans for it, I announced those plans to anyone who came to visit. I spoke of it as if I already had the money in the bank.

One morning as I was driving to work, I saw a building that was "For Lease" just two blocks from my home. Up to this point, the building had been used as a warehouse and in my assessment was perfect for a recording studio. Every morning on my way to my old studio, I would see the building and visualize it as my new studio.

The absurdity was that I had no money in my pocket and yet here I was, dreaming of a new studio!

Games Business People Play

In the early 90s, a major record label and a client of mine, who was an independent record label owner, were trying to negotiate a deal for the sale of my client's record company. They had worked together for several years and successfully contributed to the development and advancement of the Tejano music industry. My client wanted out of the business and offered to sell his company to the major label.

The major label was not willing to pay my client's asking price, so he informed them that if they were not interested in buying it, another major record company would. Thinking my client was bluffing, the major label pulled away from the negotiations. Within two days, my client's company *was*, in fact, sold to another major label, for several million dollars. That first major label made a bad business decision by calling my client's bluff, which caused them to miss out on a product line that had been very successful for them.

As representatives for the major record label that lost out on the deal regrouped to see what could be done to minimize the damage, someone in the room suggested, "Why not approach Manny Guerra and hire him exclusively? After all, he's the one that has been producing the music for the label anyway." They then invited me to meet with them and shortly thereafter "made me an offer I couldn't refuse." The major label's focus and intent was to sign me to an exclusive contract in order to distance me from my previous client. As result of signing the contract, the new recording studio that had to that point only been a dream, became a reality within two years.

Manny 1990

Opportunities to Cast the Seed of His Word

After relocating my recording studio to its new and last location, I received a telephone call from a dear friend who had been the first dance promoter in the Dallas area to book The Fabulous Sunglows. Ultimately, he became prominent in the music business via the creation of one of the biggest Tejano record labels in that area, which had an extended outreach to California and many other states. Some time in the early '70s, shortly after surrendering my life to God, I had specifically taken a trip to Dallas for the sole purpose of sharing my spiritual experience with him. After listening to my testimony, he mentioned that he knew what I was talking about because he had been raised by Christian parents who were still members of an evangelical church. I had not seen nor spoken with him since that meeting. Now, he was calling to see if I could help him make contact with an evangelist who had also been a popular musician. My friend seemed quite upset that the evangelist was not returning his calls. I explained that he was probably very busy ministering the Word of God. I asked if there was anything I could do to help. He began to share that he had hit rock bottom and had lost all his businesses, all of his possessions, and now had some serious personal problems. All he wanted was to reach out to this evangelist for prayer. I advised him that I would be glad and willing to assist him. He responded, "Would you?" Without hesitation, I answered, "Absolutely! What do you say I take a flight in the morning and visit with you? Would you pick me up at the airport?" He agreed.

I arrived in Dallas the next morning. We stopped at a local restaurant, where I shared God's plan of salvation. We prayed and he received the "gift" of salvation through faith in Jesus Christ. I called a dear pastor I knew in Dallas and advised him that a gentleman I was sitting with "has *just* submitted his life to our Savior Jesus Christ and will be in need of guidance and discipling. Can you help?" "Of course!" he responded. This newly-converted former dance promoter went on to became one of the most successful "witnesses" of the power of God, not only in the Dallas area but at the numerous cities where Tejano music had proven to be well-known and popular.

Several years after that, I was invited to speak at this dear brother's 72nd birthday celebration and happily learned that his entire family had also received Jesus Christ as their personal Lord and Savior and were actively witnessing for our Lord. This is a perfect example of God enlightening, softening, and preparing a heart to receive His word or seed. As Christians, we are to be obedient to God by freely spreading or sowing His seed, i.e., sharing the Word with everyone we come in contact. It is only God's providence and power that cultivates, germinates, and grows the seed. Praise God for His goodness and love.

Enter the Major Record Companies

During the early 90s, major record labels had begun investing and had become a major force in the Tejano music industry. However, these major investors likely misread the Spanish music market when they failed to realize how diversified and widespread that market was. Spanish music was emerging from Mexico, Cuba, Central and South America, all in addition to our local Tejano music market. It took some time, but the major record labels finally understood that the Tejano music market was very small and limited in scope and that it predominantly only appealed to Hispanics in Texas. After coming to this realization, they began to pull out from the Tejano music industry, releasing artists from their recording contracts as they exited. This trend served to deal a blow to the genre that would eventually prove fatal. While at the time of this writing some interest in Tejano music still exists, for all intents and purposes, its "heyday" is now a thing of the past. Whether the genre will ever experience a resurgence of mass interest has yet to be determined.

Successful Business and Goodness of God

In 1993, I made a decision to sign a distribution agreement with WEA Latina, a subsidiary of Time-Warner. The agreement was good for our business, which at that point, was flourishing. But still, as before, I continued to experience an emptiness or void that no amount of success and money could fill. Regardless, I continued to work hard.

Manny 1993

Record Producer of the Year

In March of 1993, I was the recipient of the "Record Producer of the Year" award at the Tejano Music Awards. It was noted that I had been a part of creating a genre that is now referred to as "Tejano Music." The award was presented by the Governor of the State of Texas at that time, the Honorable Ann Richards. I accepted the award on behalf of the countless people whose names are not known to Tejano music lovers; musicians, writers, and artists who contributed their time and dedicated efforts to establishing the genre and making it as successful as it had become. At the time and retrospectively, I never could get over the thought and the irony that a part of the birth of Tejano Music had taken place in a "one-track, hole-in-the-wall" recording studio on the south side of San Antonio.

Former Texas Governor Ann Richards

Tejano Music Awards 1993

Manny

13th Annual Tejano Music Awards Manny R.
Guerra Record Producer of The Year
Friday March 12, 1993 San Antonio, Texas Tejano Music Award

Walking and Talking

One day in mid-1995 as I was exercising (walking) at the local high school track, I took the opportunity to thank God for His love and mercy toward me. I thanked Him for the many opportunities He had granted me in life...but I remained curious about some things. My questions to God included:

Father, most of my adult life I have lived in disobedience to you. That is not what I wanted but that is certainly how I lived.

You are all-knowing. If you knew I was going to spend most of my life unsuccessfully trying to live according to your calling and was going to fail in the process, why did you even bother with me?

What I am asking is, "Why did I fail so miserably at this?"

At that moment, I felt every ounce of the failure that I was. Finally, mournful and humbled because of my sins and failures (*as the Bible says we should be before we can come to the Lord*), I prayed, "Lord, Your Word says that 'if we confess our sins, you are faithful and just to forgive us our sins and cleanse us from all unrighteousness.' I did it before and I am going to take you at your word again. I repent of all my sins and accept your forgiveness...but this time, unlike the previous times, I want you to take the reins, Lord. You haven't failed me, not one time! All of my failures at this have been because I have not totally given myself over to you. I've kept trying to do things my way and not your way. I have experienced worldly sorrow, which leads to failure and death, instead of Godly sorrow, which leads to salvation and eternal life. I have tried to earn salvation through good works, which is impossible for any person to do, because we are saved through faith. And this is not our own doing; it is the gift of God, not a result of works, so that no one may boast." (Ephesians 2:8) That is why I keep falling away! *That day, unlike the Sunday in June of 1968*, was *truly* "the beginning of the rest of my life." Therefore, if anyone is in Christ, he is a new creation. The old has passed away; behold, the new has come. (2 Corinthians 5:17) So shall my word be that goes out from my mouth; it shall not return to Me empty, but it shall accomplish that which I purpose, and shall succeed in the thing for which I sent it. (Isaiah 55:11) The "seed" that my precious mother had consistently sown for close to nine years proved what God says is true: "It shall not return to [Him] empty." I am not capable of maintaining a walk with you; only you can accomplish that! Take me, mold me, and make me into the person you want me to be!" I was three blocks away from the recording studio, where I went, sat at the front office desk, and began confessing all of my sins. It went on for quite a while, then the floodgates burst open. I had never wept as much as I did that evening; I thought it would never end.

I could hardly wait to get home and share the news with my wife. However, as I shared, it seemed as if my words weren't registering with her. I then realized that I had been so double-minded in the past, (as James 1:8 states "a double-minded man, unstable in all his ways), trying to serve God one moment and turning my back on Him the next, no one believed me anymore. My employees did not believe it either...until a month later, when I announced that I was selling all of my interests in the secular music business.

I kept my word to continue to produce for the major record label for the length of our agreement, then I would be out of the secular music world completely. Many continued to persistently argue that there was nothing wrong with secular music, that it was just a business and that it was how I was supposed to make a living. I had listened to this reasoning for too long; it would stop here! I had peace in my heart knowing I would finally no longer have a part in creating and promoting music that does not glorify God.

Musical Goliath Laid to Rest

No more than a month later, my wife Rosalinda and I decided to sell all of our business interests in the secular music world. We sold the music publishing company to Universal Publishing and our record company to EMI Capitol, a division of Capitol Records. We amicably severed all relationships with the secular music world and have since lived by faith in Jesus Christ. This time, I not only weakened, stunned, or injured the giant, in the name of Jesus, I dealt him a fatal blow that would eliminate his presence in my life permanently. All praise to God!

After selling our music publishing business and record label, we dedicated ourselves to exclusively recording gospel music. At the time of this writing, I am producing six different ministries that travel throughout the US and several Latin American countries.

Manny 1994

Faith & Reasoning

In the late 90's, my brother Rudy informed me that God wanted him to spend a whole year in Guatemala, evangelizing. I immediately felt the need to sit him down and give him "a good talking to." I said, "Rudy, you have children you must support. The believers in Guatemala don't have the same opportunities we have in America. They don't have enough income to support themselves, much less provide for your needs while you are there. You won't be able to make ends meet." He sat there and listened. All he said was, "I wonder if God knows this."

That year, Rudy's supporters in the U.S. provided him with more help than they had ever given to his ministry. This is a perfect example of the faulty and limited reasoning of man versus the goodness and wisdom of God.

Tragedy & God's Mercy

During the first week of September 1997, while dismissing some musicians who had been working with me on a project, the phone rang. I answered and the voice said, "I am calling to tell you that Becky's brother was involved in an accident." (Becky is my wife's daughter; my stepdaughter). When the voice said *Becky's brother*, I assumed it was one of Becky's other three brothers.

So, I asked, "Which one of the boys was in the accident?"

The voice answered, "The little one."

There was no "little one" except Jonathan, my wife's and my son. "Jonathan!?" I asked.

"Yes," the voice responded.

"Where did this happen?"

"On the street that leads to your recording studio," she answered.

As I looked out the front door, I saw an ambulance, police cars, and fire trucks. I immediately hung up the telephone and rushed across the street. As I made my way through the crowd, I saw my nine-year-old son, his head covered with a towel soaked with blood, lying in the middle of the street. My heart sank. It was like a horrible nightmare. Jonathan was moaning and did not know where he was.

As the medics placed him on the gurney, I heard people asking other people, "What happened?" I heard one of them say, "See
that van over there? The rear wheel of that van ran over his head."
I thought at that moment that I would lose my mind. They placed
Jonathan into the ambulance and the driver asked me where I wanted
them to take him. I responded, "The nearest hospital is about two
miles away. Let's take him there." The driver said, "They don't have
a trauma staff there. It would be better to take him to Wilford Hall
Hospital. They can do more for him there." I immediately agreed.

Sometime after Jonathan was taken into the emergency room, a
doctor came out to the waiting area and told us that he was in *critical*
condition. My wife, step-daughter Becky, and I waited, praying that
God would help us through this. My heart was even heavier seeing
my wife go through all the pain that only a mother can experience. I
comforted them both, advising them to place their trust in the Lord.
What else could we do? I added, "We are at God's mercy. He is the
only one who can help us through this." About forty-five minutes
later, which seemed like an eternity, the doctor came out and told us
that they were going to give Jonathan a CAT scan to see if there were
any serious head injuries. Then they would take him for X-rays to see
if any bones were broken.

After another agonizing hour, the specialist who performed the
procedures gave us this report: "Your son is very fortunate. There
are no serious head injuries or broken bones. The rear bumper of
the vehicle apparently pulled part of his scalp back. We cleaned the
wound and sutured the scalp back in place. He will have some scars
on top of his head but when his hair grows out, you will not be able
to see them." The doctor said, "We will wait and see how he reacts
when he wakes up." Three days later, Jonathan awoke and asked for
something to drink. He didn't remember anything about the accident. Two days later, we were able to take him home. Praise God
Almighty!

Regardless of the outcomes, God ordains or allows suffering in the
believer's life to develop and strengthen dependence on Him and to
create perseverance in us. "Count it all joy, my brothers, when you
meet trials of various kinds, for you know that the testing of your

faith produces steadfastness" (James 1:2-3). As Christians, we are not immune to the trials and sufferings of this physical world and life, but unlike unbelievers, people that put their trust in God have a joyful peace that is foreign to our earthly human nature. "Peace I leave with you. My peace I give you. I give you not as the world gives. Do not be troubled or afraid" (John 14:27). Only genuine belief and sincere trust in God and His sovereign plan can provide unspeakable peace and understanding during our darkest hours.

Heart Problems (Physically)

In September of 2005, I began to experience a pain in the middle of my back. It had been going on for a couple of weeks and the only relief I would get was when I rolled up a face towel, placed it on the floor, and laid on it. My wife advised me to see the doctor two blocks down the street to get some x-rays but I told her, "I haven't been to see a doctor in twenty years." She insisted, "Go and let him take an x-ray." I finally listened to her and went.

The medical assistant checked my vitals several times, then said, "Wait here for a moment; I am going to get the doctor."

The doctor walked in and I said, "What's going on doctor? You guys are going to give me a heart attack."

He responded, "Stay calm for a few minutes."

After they placed me in their "trauma room," I kept asking the doctor, "What's going on?"

He said, "We are not able to lower your blood pressure. Are you feeling faint or short of breath? Do you have an upset stomach?"

I said, "No, I feel fine."

He said, "Your blood pressure is 204/104. You should be having a very bad headache right about now."

I responded, "*I don't.*"

He said, "We are calling an ambulance and transporting you to the hospital."

I immediately countered with, "*Hold on!* There's no need for that. I can drive myself there."

He said, "Sorry, I can't do that. I am responsible for you now."

The following day a cardiologist conducted some tests and found that an artery on the backside of my heart was 95% clogged. I would need to undergo a procedure to insert a "stent." I asked the doctor if it was serious. He answered, "What you have is known as the 'silent killer.' The artery could rupture and you would go in your sleep." He added, "If you had this condition on the front-side of your heart instead of where it is, we wouldn't be talking right now." The stent procedure was successful and thanks to God, I was able to continue my life journey.

Music: Good or Bad?

As has been clearly presented throughout this document, music has been in the center of my life since I was an infant. Throughout the years, I used the recording studio as my isolation space, with music as my support system. My brother Rudy and I would often joke about me spending all of my time in "the cave." I spent close to 60 years there, immersed in music. I considered music to be the glue that held all things together for me. Music was a place of refuge for whatever situation I was going through in life. If I was happy, I listened to music that made me happier. If I was sad, I played music that matched my sadness and oftentimes, intensified it. Regardless of the situation, music was "my space." Before long and unbeknownst to me, it came to be my crutch.

The singing and playing of numerous musical instruments were practiced by the Israelites all the way back to Genesis, the very first book of the Bible. Music was used in sacred processions, consecration of temples, coronation of kings, victory celebrations, and religious feasts. However, music also found use as private entertainment and in idol and demon worshipping. This represents yet another instance where Satan took something that God created for good and twisted it toward the negative or sinful mode.

Christ wants us to completely submit our lives to Him, immerse ourselves in His Word on a daily basis, and reap the benefits of a sanctified walk with Him while here on earth, followed by a glorious eternal life in His presence. Because our daily walk with Him requires our full attention and dedication, *anything* that distracts from our thoughts and focused time with Him is considered a hindrance, often progressing to the status of an idol, which is Biblically described as "*anything* that comes between God and us." After all of my years in the music business, I have come to see and understand that is actually what secular music became in my life: a consuming idol and obstacle between me and God.

While many will argue that there is nothing wrong with the various genres of music, we must be mindful of the lyrics that we mindlessly listen to, learn, repeat, and sometimes, unbeknownst to ourselves, apply to our daily lives. They have a direct and negative effect on our thoughts, which further impact our moods, attitudes, and hearts. Anything that is not inspired by and for God can only have been inspired, created, and used by Satan. "Set your minds on things that are above, not on things that are on earth" (Colossians 3:2) and "Whether you eat or drink or *whatever you do*, do it all for the glory of God" (1 Corinthians 10:31).

I write and advise this directly from my experiences. Satan used music to occupy my mind and distract me from precious time with God; time that I could have otherwise dedicated to learning more about Him. Relative to music, the focus should be on music that promotes and glorifies God; that is what we should immerse our thoughts and minds with, focusing on our Creator and Savior as He has directed us through His Scriptures. "Let the word of Christ dwell in you richly, teaching and admonishing one another in all wisdom, *singing psalms and hymns and spiritual songs*, with thankfulness in your hearts to God" (Colossians 3:16).

FACEBOOK

I asked God if the knowledge He had graciously allowed me to understand was for my benefit only and if I would take it to the grave with me? That is when he led me to discover the medium of Facebook.

I use Facebook on a daily basis to share many thoughts, and insights about God and His glorious plan for those who come to believe in Him as Lord and Savior. Facebook provides me with a platform that can reach people who seldom, if ever, have the opportunity to hear the message of salvation elsewhere.

After my first year and a half on Facebook, I would see a few people responding with "likes" and even less people with "comments." I remember praying and asking God, "Is this Facebook a tool of Yours or is it something I conjured up? Whosever idea it is, it does not seem to be having much success."

A couple of weeks later, a precious fellow-believer from Redondo Beach, California, contacted me to tell me that quite a few people were reading my posts. I loved this brother dearly but I figured he was just trying to encourage me. I could see that the numbers on my Facebook page didn't align with what he was saying. Two weeks later, I received a "Congratulatory" post directly from Facebook, advising me that multiple-thousands of people had read my posts. It encouraged me to continue spreading the Good News of God and His Son, Jesus Christ via the medium God had provided.

I will never again question Father God concerning what avenues I should pursue in announcing His "Good News." I will use any and all that are made available to me, in order to fulfill the "Great Commission" Jesus commanded His disciples.

Lessons Learned from My Life

Below, I have provided information on the steps necessary for accepting the gift of salvation through the Savior, Jesus Christ. Based on what you have read about my life to this point, your first reaction could/should be:

Why would I listen to you on such matters? Your life certainly wasn't a picture of consistency, dedication, or spiritual success!

And from a purely humanistic perspective, your reasoning and reaction would certainly be correct and warranted. However, before you close the book and discontinue reading, here are some thoughts for you to ponder.

I came to the Lord in 1968 but as you've read, I veered from the walk with Him...multiple, multiple times. *Why?* Pure and simple, it was because, instead of me completely humbling myself before God and letting *Him* make the necessary changes to my heart from the inside- out...like it's supposed to be, I *proudly* came to Him and tried to make changes to myself...on my own, from the outside-in. I tried to do God's work by changing my human reasoning, logic, and associated actions, but my sinful heart remained, unchanged; unredeemed. When I finally came to His feet, "at my wit's end," humbled, repentant, and open to allowing *Him* to make the necessary changes to my sinful heart that He deemed necessary, *only then* did real, genuine, and life-altering changes take place. The amazing thing about God is that throughout, He had patience with me until He deemed the Holy Spirit to help me realize the error of my ways and thinking. He was patient, faithful, and caring and He accepted and welcomed me into the family of believers without hesitation.

I will be the first to admit...and the information provided in this book supports this premise...that my life-walk, in so many instances, gives you, the reader, perfect examples of what *NOT* to do! However, (even though it took me 30 years to realize and understand it!), my life also provides an example of what *should* be done, in that it clearly provides clear and unmistakable evidence of a God who is patient and faithful, who graciously cares about you, loves you, and is mercifully persistent in wanting us to avoid judgment. 2 Peter 3:9 says, "The Lord is not slow in keeping His promise, as some understand slowness. Instead, He is patient with you, not wanting anyone to perish, but everyone to come to repentance." My veering from the "straight and narrow" path with God cost me special times with my family and loved ones...but most importantly, I lost precious, tender moments with God that I cannot make up for in this life. I certainly pray that doesn't become a reality for you.

In this book, I have shared what many would consider private matters and events that most people would be reluctant to divulge to the reading public. I have been completely open and transparent about both my very public and my very private life. Why would I do such a thing? Two reasons:

- To bring honor and glory to God by showing His faithfulness in rescuing me, "in that while we were still (prideful) sinners, Christ died for us." (Romans 5:8) and
- Because I remain hopeful that if something...*anything*...in my life could serve to prompt and bring souls to personally know the saving and redeeming grace of God, then my efforts and my sharing were not in vain.

In Matthew 22:37-39, Christ commanded us to "Love the Lord your God with all of your heart and with all your soul and with all your mind" and you shall "Love your neighbor as yourself." *You,* the reader, are my neighbor. *You* are the person and the reason these memoirs were written. *You* are the soul for whom God is reaching out to and for. He said, "Behold, I stand at the door and knock. If anyone hears my voice and opens the door, I will come in and eat with him and he with Me." (Revelation 3:20).

There are many people, causes, ideologies, plans, and programs that claim to offer life to its fullest here on earth and some, even into the afterlife...*but don't you believe it!* Jesus said, "I am the way, the truth, and the life. *No one* comes to the Father except through Me" (John 14:6). I truly believe that the quote that says "God uses the first half of our life to show us how to live the last half of it" has been true and accurate in my life. I trust and pray that God will be an intimate, vital, and centermost part of each of your lives here in this temporary world, so you can spend eternity in His loving and glorious presence in the permanent world to come.

The Background

As our Creator, God created us to enjoy fellowship with Him.

- "So God created man in His own image; in the image of God He created him; male and female He created them." (Genesis 1:27)

The Bad News

When mankind sinned (in Genesis, chapter 3), it caused a separation or rift between God and mankind. Since then, all mankind is born with a sinful nature at birth; no exceptions!

- "For all have sinned and come short of the glory of God" (Romans 3:23).
- "If we say that we have no sin, we are deceiving ourselves and the truth is not in us" (1 John 1:8)
- "If we say that we have not sinned, we make Him a liar and His word is not in us" (1 John 1:10)

The separation or rift cannot be avoided, regardless of how nice or good of a person you think you are, because our natures are sinful and God is pure and holy and His nature cannot tolerate sin. The two cannot mix.

The bad news is because of our sinfulness, we deserve death.

Many people don't understand or accept that because we are in sin, that *automatically* makes us enemies of God, regardless of how nice or good a person we may think we are!

- "For all have sinned and fall short of the glory of God" (Romans 3:23) and
- "None is righteous, no, not one. No one understands; no one seeks for God (Romans 3:10-11) and
- "The wages of sin is death…" (Romans 6:23)

The worse news is we can't save ourselves; no matter how hard we try to make amends! No matter how good we can try to be or act! Spiritually, we are not capable of paying for and ridding ourselves of sin. That premise is painfully obvious and repeatedly on display throughout these memoirs.

The Good News

The good news exists only because of God's love, kindness, goodness, and mercy that even though He was the offended party (i.e., because we have sinned against Him!), God *Himself* created a soul-saving route for us! Here's how He accomplished that:

- "For God so loved the world that He gave His only Son, that whosoever believes in Him should not perish but have eternal life" (John 3:16).
- "For our sake, He (God) made Him (Jesus) to be sin that knew no sin, so that in Him (Jesus) we might become the righteousness of God" (2 Corinthians 5:21).
  - Jesus provided the link or the bridge we needed to reach or access God!
- Yes, "The wages of sin is death (as noted above) but the gift of God is eternal life through Jesus Christ our Lord!" (Romans 6:23)

The Appropriate Actions and Reactions

The Good News, i.e., the way-out that God has created for us is not automatic; it requires concrete, meaningful, and determined commitment and action on each of our parts.

- You must admit that you are as sinner (as explained above)
- You must repent from your sins.
  - Repenting is the equivalent of retreating; it is a 180° turnaround.

○ "Repent and turn from all of your transgressions, so that iniquity will not be your ruin. Cast away from you all the transgressions which you have committed and get yourselves a new heart and a new spirit" (Ezekiel 18:30-31).

- You must confess.
  ○ You must confess (tell) all your sins *to God*; He, alone, has the power to cleanse you from that sin, through the blood of His Son, Jesus Christ.
  ○ "If we confess our sins, He is faithful and just to forgive us our sins, and to cleanse us from all unrighteousness." (1 John 1:9)

- You must believe by faith.
  ○ "For by grace you have been saved through faith, and that not of yourselves; it is the gift of God" (Ephesians 2:8).
  ○ "But as many as received Him, to them He gave power to become the sons of God, even to them that believe on His name." (John 1:12)

Prayer of Repentance

If you desire to be forgiven of all your sins and spend eternity with God, you can simply pray this simple prayer of "repentance."

> Dear God, I understand that I was born a sinner. I confess my sins and repent of them all. I believe with all my heart that your Son Jesus Christ died on a cruel cross to pay my debt of sin. I believe that He died, was buried, and you raised Him from the dead, and He lives forever to intercede on my behalf. I receive Jesus Christ as my Lord and Savior and receive the person of the Holy Spirit, who enlightens me, comforts me, and seals me until the day of His return. Thank you for my salvation, Father God. Help me to live for you. In Jesus' name. Amen.

The Bible says "if you confess with your mouth that Jesus is Lord and believe in your heart that God raised him from the dead, you will be saved" (Romans 10:9).

So, if you verbally prayed this prayer and believed in your heart, through faith in Jesus Christ, you are now a child of God, a member of God's household, and a citizen of God's Kingdom. Praise God!

The Necessary Reactions (on our part)

When we *sincerely* and *truly* become Christians, our lives and the way we live are changed forever. Our old ways cease to exist and new patterns develop.

- "Therefore, if anyone is in Christ, he is a new creation. The old has passed away; behold, the new has come" (2 Corinthians 5:17).

We begin to bear the fruits of repentance:

- "By this my Father is glorified, that you bear much fruit and so prove to be my disciples." (John 15:8)

True Christians still sin…but not like before. Sinful habits and continuous indulgences in sinful behaviors become repulsive to a heart fill with faith and love for Christ. Sins are progressively negated and neutralized in lives of believers who place God in the center of their hearts and lives. When the Savior sits on the throne of one's heart, there *has to be* a change!

- "No one born of God makes a practice of sinning, for God's seed abides in him, and he cannot keep on sinning because he has been born of God." (1 John 3:9)
- "And by this we know that we have come to know him, if we keep His commandments. Whoever says, "I know Him,

but does not keep His commandments is a liar, and the truth is not in him." (1 John 2:3-4)

If we *genuinely* repent and trust in Christ, righteous Christian-like changes *do* occur. As mentioned, the difference of what led to my backslides versus my later committed, consistent, and fulfilling walk with Christ is that ultimately, I had to *truly, sincerely, and genuinely* give my heart over to Him, taking my hands off of the reins and letting Him make changes from the inside-out, not from the outside-in, like I was trying to accomplish on my own power. We cannot be saved via any good works we might conjure up. We can only be saved by the blessed blood of Jesus Christ, who changes hearts *and lives.*

A heart that is changed and filled with God's presence will willingly and eagerly seek to have fellowship with Him, will *want* to follow Christ's direction on how we are to view and obey Him, and how we are to view and behave with others. As mentioned earlier, we are to love the Lord God with all our heart, soul, mind, and body and we are to love our neighbors as yourselves. These are not options; they are commands. However, "His commandments are not burdensome" (1 John 5:3). God's spirit, presence, and love in our hearts makes us *want* to love and serve Him, as well as our fellow humans. The purpose of man's existence on this earth can only be truly fulfilled when we come to know God...and that can only be learned and attained through the study and application of His Holy Scriptures.

The Bible / The Word of God

A manufacturer, be it of automobiles, washing machines, or audio/video equipment, always includes a *manual* with instructions on how to use the respective device. The manuals explain *what the creator of the particular device or equipment designed it to do.*

In much the same way, *The Bible* is God's manual with instructions on what the Creator of life had in mind when He created man. If we follow the teachings of our Lord, Jesus Christ, we will find peace with God. If we don't, we will live miserable lives without direction and without purpose.

God chose to reveal Himself and speak to mankind through *all* sixty-six books comprising the Bible, divided into the Old and New Testament. For those uninformed souls who think the Bible is just another book, know that "All Scripture is breathed out of God and profitable for teaching, for reproof, for correction, and for training in righteousness (2 Timothy 3:16).

For those who may be ill-informed and ill-advised thinking that the Word of God is outdated, is no longer applicable, and has out-lived its usefulness or is obsolete, we know that Jesus said "Heaven and earth will pass away but my words will not pass away" (Mark 31:13) and "...it is easier for heaven and earth to pass away than for one dot of the Law to become void" (Luke 16:17). So we can confidently conclude that the Word of God will out-live life on this earth and into eternity.

The Bible, also referred to as the Word of God, is all we need for a right relationship with God. The Spirit of God, acting through the Word of God, is sufficient and all anyone needs to fully mature in Christ; *no other added spiritual or mystical experiences necessary.* We don't need a vision, a new revelation, or a voice from heaven. God, through His Omniscient (all-knowing) and Omnipotent (all-powerful) sovereign plan has provided all of the wisdom, revelation, direction, guidance, assistance, information, and prophesy we need to successfully guide us through this life, in preparation for an eternal life with Him. The Bible is perfect because it contains the words of a perfect God. The best way to think of the Scriptures is to remember that "Whatever the Scriptures say, God said."

Any person with a heart that is cleansed, redeemed, and justified by faith in Jesus Christ as their personal Lord and Savior, along with the enlightenment, clarification, revelation, and guidance of the Holy Spirit, can grow into a sanctified Christian walk with God by reading, studying, learning, and most importantly, applying the Word of God to every facet of our daily lives. Effective study of the Word of God is basic to the Christian life. Our understanding of God and our place in His creation revolves around our knowledge of God's Word. All that is required for us to learn is desire, constant diligence, and prayer.

Time is of the Essence

God, the Creator of the Universe, through the work of the Holy Spirit, patiently waits for lost souls to turn from their prideful, sinful, and selfish ways toward the saving grace provided through His Son, Jesus Christ. Every passing day, every second, every breath, every heartbeat gets each of us one instant closer to either a glorious eternity with Him or a dreadful existence without Him. Please don't delay. Make a decision for the Lord today. Your eternal destination hangs in the balance.

My Sincere Hope

I remain hopeful this humble document will serve as a resource and blessing to those I have had the pleasure of crossing professional and personal paths with along the way as well as with those I have not yet had the privilege of meeting. My intent is solely to bring honor and glory to Almighty God and to help anyone I can toward an eternity with our Lord and Savior, Jesus Christ.

I *did not* set out to insult or harm anyone...and if I have, you have my most sincere apologies. I *did*, however, set out to offer my varied and extreme life experiences in the hopes that God would use them to bring others to the knowledge of His saving grace for mankind. If that occurs...*even with one person*...then, Praise God, this document has served its intended purpose.

CPSIA information can be obtained
at www.ICGtesting.com
Printed in the USA
BVHW032123101221
623803BV00001B/3